Q 1

Psychology

Q 2

Define behavior as it relates to psychology.

Q 3

_____ are defined as internal experiences, including feelings and thoughts.

Q 4

Why is psychology a scientific study?

Q 5

An example of the nature vs. nurture controversy is whether intelligence derives from _____ or is _____.

Q 6

What is monism?

Q 7

Plato and Descartes, believers in dualism, are on the side of _____ in the nature vs. nurture controversy.

Q 8

Aristotle, Hobbes, and Locke (believers in monism) are on the side of _____ in the nature vs. nurture controversy.

A 1 Psychology is the scientific study of behavior and mental processes.	A 2 observable actions
A 3 Mental processes	A 4 uses empirical data to test hypotheses / describes predicts and explains behavior and mental processes / systematic collection and interpretation of data
A 5 experience inherited	A 6 the idea that the brain and the mind are the same things and that every mental state is reducible to an identical brain state
A 7 nature / Descartes believed knowledge was innate and the pineal gland was considered the mind.	A 8 nurture / Locke's "tabula rasa" translates to "blank slate" suggesting that knowledge is learned through experience.

Q 9	Q 10
Did psychology grow out of which discipline(s) in Ancient Greece?	introspection

Q 11	Q 12
_____ was the first woman to receive her Ph.D. in psychology.	Who was Mary Whiton Calkins?

Q 13	Q 14
Name three of the earliest functionalists.	What theory did William James found?

Q 15	Q 16
Behavior results from learning through experience.	What is behavior modification?

A 9	A 10
philosophy physiology and biology	Introspection is the process whereby observers look inward and objectively analyze their sensory experience.
A 11	**A 12**
Margaret Floy Washburn	first female president of the American Psychological Association (APA)
A 13	**A 14**
William James / James Cattell / John Dewey	James is the founder of the functionalist perspective.
A 15	**A 16**
behavioral	set of techniques to help individuals unlearn habits that have led to psychological problems

Q 17

Describe Ivan Pavlov's classical conditioning experiments.

Q 18

What did John Watson believe psychology should study?

Q 19

Who is the psychologist behind operant conditioning of rats and pigeons?

Q 20

operant conditioning

Q 21

Max Wertheimer, Wolfgang Kohler, and Kurt Koffka were _____ psychologists.

Q 22

Where do behavioral geneticists believe behavior comes from?

Q 23

Who is the father of psychoanalysis?

Q 24

According to psychoanalysis, early life experiences are related to the development of one's _____ later in life.

A 17	A 18
Pavlov an early behaviorist in his famous classical conditioning experiment trained dogs to salivate in response to the sound of a bell.	Watson one of the earliest behaviorists felt psychology should be the science of overt behavior and reject the study of mental processes.
A 19	A 20
B.F. Skinner	training organisms to repeat responses that lead to rewards and not to repeat responses that lead to punishment
A 21	A 22
Gestalt	particular behaviors are attributed to genetically-based psychological characteristics
A 23	A 24
Sigmund Freud	personality

Q 25

Other than Sigmund Freud, name four psychologists who associate with the psychoanalytic perspective.

Q 26

The _____ approach studies unconscious motives, while the biological approach studies chemical processes.

Q 27

What is the difference between the conscious mind and the subconscious mind?

Q 28

repression

Q 29

_____, unlike behaviorists, believe free will guides behavior and leads to personal growth.

Q 30

humanism

Q 31

Name two psychologists who associate with the humanistic approach.

Q 32

Technological advances and physiological research formed the basis of the _____ approach.

A 25	A 26
Carl Jung / Alfred Adler / Karen Horney / Heinz Kohut	psychoanalytic / The psychoanalytic approach is also known as the psychodynamic approach.
A 27	A 28
The conscious mind is readily accessible while the subconscious mind is inaccessible but influences behavior.	the psychoanalytic term for burying information in the subconscious
A 29	A 30
Humanists	the psychological perspective that believes humans have unique qualities of behavior that differ from other organisms
A 31	A 32
Abraham Maslow / Carl Rogers	biological / The biological approach is also known as biopsychology or neuroscience.

Q 33

According to the biological perspective, the behavior is related to the _____ processes within the nervous and endocrine systems.

Q 34

Behaviors that contribute to survival and reproduction are naturally selected.

Q 35

Who was the inspiration behind the evolutionary approach to psychology?

Q 36

Which psychological approach focuses on thinking, language, and how humans receive, store, and process information?

Q 37

Who first studied the cognitive development of children?

Q 38

The structuralists studied consciousness, thinking, and memory. This area of psychology is currently known as _____.

Q 39

People from different cultures interpret gestures, body language, and verbal language differently.

Q 40

Name three Ancient Greeks who were philosophers who also discussed psychological concepts.

A 33	A 34
chemical	evolutionary
A 35	A 36
Charles Darwin / Darwin's theory of natural selection said all creatures have evolved to survive and reproduce.	cognitive
A 37	A 38
Jean Piaget	cognition
A 39	A 40
sociocultural / These psychologists study how cultural differences affect behavior.	Socrates / Plato / Aristotle

Q 41

Which Scientific Revolution-era thinker discussed mind-body dualism in his philosophical writings?

Q 42

_____ believed that thought and knowledge are not innate and that a human being is born as a tabula rasa.

Q 43

Who was one of the first thinkers to suggest that our perceptions of sensation are all that we can be sure of?

Q 44

_____ was an Enlightenment-era thinker who believed we were active shapers of our worlds with inborn traits that skew our perceptions.

Q 45

_____ was a Viennese scientist who was the first to use hypnotism (which he called _____) to cure mental illness.

Q 46

Phrenology, the "science" that proposed people's personalities were based on their skull shape, was created by _____.

Q 47

Who was the first psychologist to use statistics in psychological research, as well as the inventor of the correlation coefficient?

Q 48

Gustav Fechner can be considered the founder of _____ because of his use of empirical techniques to study psychological phenomena.

A 41	A 42
Rene Descartes	John Locke
A 43	**A 44**
Thomas Hobbes	Immanuel Kant
A 45	**A 46**
Anton Mesmer Mesmerism / Braid Charcot and Freud were other pioneering users of hypnosis and hypnotic techniques.	Franz Joseph Gall
A 47	**A 48**
Sir Francis Galton	experimental psychology

Q 49

eugenics

Q 50

Who wrote "Elements of Physiology," a book that suggested the existence of special nerve energies?

Q 51

The first accepted psychological laboratory was founded in 1879 by Wilhelm Wundt at _____ to study consciousness.

Q 52

Which psychologist based his work on the now-discredited evolutionary work of Lamarck, and suggested that different races passed on their intelligence to future generations?

Q 53

Who was one of the founders of our current psychology of perception?

Q 54

Who did his psychological work on the reflex arc, which proposed that animals always adapt to their environments, rather than respond to stimuli with concrete responses?

Q 55

_____ was the inventor of structuralism, and he also used introspection to examine consciousness.

Q 56

James Cattell founded psychological research laboratories in both _____ and _____, he was one of the forefathers of the experimental movement in American psychology.

A 49 a biological plan based loosely on genetics that hoped to breed human beings to create the perfect human selectively.	A 50 Johannes Muller- his theory suggested that nerves will always fire the same way despite different types of stimulation.
A 51 University of Leipzig	A 52 Herbert Spencer
A 53 Hermann von Helmholtz	A 54 John Dewey
A 55 Edward Titchener	A 56 University of Pennsylvania Columbia University

Q 57

Who was one of the founders of the American movement to provide better care for the mentally ill?

Q 58

Who created the law of effect, which eventually led to operant conditioning?

Q 59

_____ was a student of Sigmund Freud who created individual psychology, the idea of the inferiority complex, and a four-type personality system.

Q 60

Which psychologist split from Sigmund Freud to go on to create analytic psychology?

Q 61

The mechanistic behavioral equation Performance = Drive x Habit is best associated with_____.

Q 62

Which behaviorist believed that learning is acquired through purposeful behavior, which he demonstrated by running rats through mazes?

Q 63

In the 1940s, psychology moved away from research and toward the practical treatment of mental illness, which was especially apparent in the emerging field of _____.

Q 64

Who was Konrad Lorenz?

A 57	A 58
Dorothea Lynde Dix	Edward Thorndike
A 59	**A 60**
Alfred Adler	Carl Gustav Jung
A 61	**A 62**
Clark Hull	Edward Tolman
A 63	**A 64**
clinical psychology	He was one of the founders of ethology who also did an extensive research with duckling imprinting

Q 65 **Who created a new form of therapy called client-centered therapy that employed unconditional positive regard?**	**Q 66** **Abraham Maslow was famous for leading humanistic psychology and creating _____.**
Q 67 **Erik Erikson proposed an eight-stage model of development that included a _____ to transition to the next stage.**	**Q 68** **_____ and many other cognitive psychologists believed that mental illness comes from bad thinking patterns, which must be treated with cognitive therapy.**
Q 69 **learning**	**Q 70** **What are the three theories for learning?**
Q 71 **Define the stimulus as it relates to classical conditioning.**	**Q 72** **Define response as it relates to classical conditioning.**

A 65	A 66
Carl Rogers	the hierarchy of needs
A 67	**A 68**
crisis	Aaron Beck
A 69	**A 70**
a relatively permanent change in behavior as a result of experience	classical conditioning / operant conditioning / cognitive learning
A 71	**A 72**
change in the environment that brings about a response	reaction to a stimulus

Q 73	Q 74
Stimuli that increase the likelihood of behavior are called _____.	When you put food in your mouth, you salivate.

Q 75	Q 76
neutral stimulus (NS)	unconditioned stimulus (UCS or US)

Q 77	Q 78
unconditioned response (UCR or UR)	conditioned response (CR)

Q 79	Q 80
How is trace conditioning timed?	How is simultaneous conditioning timed?

A 73	A 74
reinforcers	stimulus: food / response: salivation

A 75	A 76
the stimulus that initially does not elicit a response until it becomes CS / Pavlov's example: / The NS is the bell because it does not produce salivation until it is paired with the food.	reflexively automatically brings about a response / Pavlov's example: / Food is the UCS because it automatically brings about salivation.

A 77	A 78
automatic involuntary reaction to the unconditioned stimulus / Pavlov's example: / The UCR is salivation because the dogs automatically salivate when they eat food.	learned response to a previously neutral stimulus / Pavlov's example: / Salivation is the CR because the dog learned to salivate in response to the bell.

A 79	A 80
the neutral stimulus is presented and then taken away before the unconditioned stimulus appears / Pavlov's example: / Bell rings followed by a long time lapse then food is presented.	neutral stimulus and unconditioned stimulus are presented together at the same time / Pavlov's example: / The bell rings and food is presented at the same time.

Q 81	Q 82
How is backward conditioning timed?	What researcher(s) were behind the Little Albert experiment?
Q 83	Q 84
Identify the UCS, UCR, CS, and CR in the Little Albert experiment.	spontaneous recovery
Q 85	Q 86
operant conditioning	How did Edward Thorndike contribute to research on operant conditioning?
Q 87	Q 88
What is instrumental learning?	What is a Skinner box?

A 81	A 82
the unconditioned stimulus is presented before the neutral stimulus / Pavlov's example: / Food is presented before the bell rings.	John B. Watson and Rosalie Rayner
A 83	**A 84**
UCS: loud noise / UCR: fear / CS: white rat / CR: fear	original response disappears and then returns later on / Pavlov's example: salivation from bell stops and then returns / Little Albert: baby stops crying from the presence of rat and then begins again
A 85	**A 86**
learning that occurs when a subject performs certain voluntary behavior and the consequences of the behavior determine the likelihood of its recurrence	put cats in puzzle boxes to demonstrate trial and error in obtaining a fish / coined the terms "instrumental learning" and "Law of Effect"
A 87	**A 88**
Thorndike's term for a type of associative learning where behavior becomes more or less probable depending on its consequence	operant conditioning chamber for research animals designed by B.F. Skinner that contained levers food dispensers lights and an electrified grid

Q 89 **What are the four training procedures of B.F. Skinner's operant conditioning?**	**Q 90** **positive reinforcement**
Q 91 **negative reinforcement**	**Q 92** **What are avoidance and escape behaviors?**
Q 93 **punishment**	**Q 94** **omission training**
Q 95 **What is aversive conditioning?**	**Q 96** **learned helplessness**

A 89 positive reinforcement / negative reinforcement / positive punishment / negative punishment	A 90 reward training where behavior is followed by a reinforcer that increases the probability that the behavior will occur again / Example: / praise after participating in class
A 91 removing an unpleasant consequence / Example: / the kid does his chores to avoid getting yelled at	A 92 avoidance behavior: takes away the aversive stimulus before it begins / escape behavior: takes away the aversive stimulus after it has already started
A 93 the unpleasant consequence that follows a voluntary behavior decreasing the probability the behavior will be repeated a.k.a. positive punishment / Example: / spanking a child for misbehaving	A 94 removing a rewarding consequence following a voluntary behavior decreasing the probability the behavior will be repeated / Example: / taking away a child's toy after misbehaving
A 95 learning that involves an unpleasant stimulus or reinforcer such as negative reinforcement and punishment	A 96 state of feeling powerless to change yourself or your situation because of a prior inability to avoid an aversive event

Q 97 **What are the three types of reinforcers?**	Q 98 **primary reinforcers**
Q 99 **secondary reinforcers**	Q 100 **generalized reinforcers**
Q 101 **How does a token economy work?**	Q 102 **Define behavior modification in terms of operant conditioning.**
Q 103 **How is shaping used to teach a new behavior?**	Q 104 **Define chaining as it relates to operant conditioning.**

A 97 primary / secondary / generalized	A 98 something that is biologically naturally important and therefore rewarding / Example: / food and drink
A 99 something neutral that can become rewarding when associated with a primary reinforcer / Examples: / gold stars tokens points money	A 100 secondary reinforcer that can be associated with several primary reinforcers / Example: / money can be used to buy food and also other enjoyable items.
A 101 operant conditioning system / secondary reinforcers are used to increase acceptable behaviors / tokens can be exchanged for privileges and prizes / used in mental hospitals and jails	A 102 small steps are rewarded until the intended goal is achieved / uses the behavioral approach to solve individual institutional and societal problems
A 103 positively reinforcing closer and closer approximations of the desired behavior / Example: / In toilet training rewards are given to the child at each step.	A 104 initially positively reinforcing each behavior in a certain order / later on rewards only given for completing the whole sequence in order to establish a specific sequence of behaviors

Q 105 **What is the purpose of reinforcement schedules?**	Q 106 **What is a continuous reinforcement schedule?**
Q 107 **What is a partial reinforcement schedule?**	Q 108 **What is a ratio schedule and what are the four types?**
Q 109 **fixed ratio schedule**	Q 110 **fixed interval schedule**
Q 111 **variable interval schedule**	Q 112 **How is superstitious behavior formed?**

A 105	A 106
to determine how and when reinforcers will be given to the learner	provides reinforcement every time the behavior is exhibited by human or animal

A 107	A 108
reinforcing behavior only some of the time / a.k.a. intermittent schedule	schedule based on the number of desired responses / fixed ratio / fixed interval / variable ratio / variable interval

A 109	A 110
reinforcement comes after a specific number of behavior responses / Example: / Every three times you get a question right you get a piece of candy.	reinforcement comes at a specific time / Example: / Having a review at a job at a specific time each year to determine compensation

A 111	A 112
amount of time before reinforcement of behavior changes / Example: / You study every night in preparation for a pop quiz because you don't know when it is coming.	When reinforcement occurs during an idiosyncratic behavior the organism is likely to repeat that behavior even though it doesn't cause the reinforcement.

Q 113	Q 114
What did John B. Watson and B.F. Skinner study?	What do cognitive theorists believe humans and other animals are capable of, beyond classical and operant conditioning?
Q 115	Q 116
What is the contingency model?	What model did the contingency model counter?
Q 117	Q 118
What is the blocking effect?	Name an example of delayed gratification.
Q 119	Q 120
Who was Edward Tolman?	latent learning

A 113	A 114
studied only behaviors disregarded thought processes because they were not observable	forming expectations and being consciously motivated by rewards
A 115	**A 116**
Richard Rescorla's theory that the key to classical conditioning is how well the CS predicts the appearance of the UCS	Pavlov's contiguity model that classical conditioning is based on the association in time of the CS prior to the UCS.
A 117	**A 118**
Leon Kamin's concept that the conditioning effect of the neutral stimulus is blocked when already conditioned with UCS	saving money for college or a car rather than spending it immediately
A 119	**A 120**
confirmed the presence of latent learning / found unrewarded rats form a cognitive map of the maze so when presented with a reward they are motivated to improve	learning in the absence of rewards

Q 121 Define insight as it relates to learning.	Q 122 Who observed insight in chimpanzees?
Q 123 observational learning	Q 124 What are the four steps of observational learning, according to Albert Bandura?
Q 125 What were the results of the bobo dolls experiment?	Q 126 What provides the biological basis for observational learning?
Q 127 Define preparedness as it relates to learning.	Q 128 Who experimented on conditioned taste aversions and biological preparedness in rats?

A 121	A 122
the sudden appearance of an answer or solution to a problem	Wolfgang Kohler
A 123	A 124
learning that occurs by watching the behavior of a model / a.k.a. social learning or vicarious learning	attention / retention / reproduction / motivation
A 125	A 126
when offered rewards to imitate violent behavior did not always lead to a response / demonstrated modeling: those who watched violent models imitated them	Mirror neurons are activated when you perform an action and when you observe someone else perform a similar action.
A 127	A 128
Through evolution animals are biologically predisposed to easily learn behaviors related to their survival as a species.	John Garcia and Robert Koelling

Q 129 What is instinctive drift?	Q 130 What is the evidence of biological factors of learning?
Q 131 What is long-term potentiation?	Q 132 What psychological school was founded by John Watson?
Q 133 What is another term for "classical conditioning"?	Q 134 What does backward conditioning cause?
Q 135 What is an alternate term for "shaping"?	Q 136 What are some primary drives for learning?

A 129 CR that drifts back toward the natural instinctive behavior of the organism	A 130 Rats raised in enriched environments had thicker cortices higher brain weight and greater neural connectivity than rats raised in deprived environments.
A 131 physiological change that correlates with a stable change in behavior due to experience / "neurons that fire together wire together" / studied by Donald Hebb and Eric Kandel	A 132 the school of behaviorism / Watson believed we learn through conditioning of stimulus-response chains.
A 133 Pavlovian conditioning	A 134 inhibitory conditioning / Inhibitory conditioning prevents forward conditioning.
A 135 differential reinforcement of successive approximations	A 136 Also known as instinctual drives primary drives include basic functions like hunger and thirst.

Q 137 **What are some secondary drives for learning?**	Q 138 **What is an exploratory drive?**
Q 139 **What does Hull's belief that performance=drive x habit mean?**	Q 140 **Explain Edward Tolman's expectancy-value theory.**
Q 141 **What did Henry Murray and David McLelland believe motivated people's behavior?**	Q 142 **According to John Atkinson, do we desire success more or fear failure more?**
Q 143 **What was Neil Miller's approach-avoidance conflict?**	Q 144 **Hedonism is the belief that behaviors are motivated by the desire to feel _____ and avoid _____.**

A 137	A 138
Secondary drives or acquired drives may include fame money or other motivators that are not instinctual.	It is neither a primary nor secondary drive and appears to be motivated simply by the desire to do or learn something novel.
A 139	A 140
People will have a drive for something then use previous behaviors that have accomplished that goal to inform their future actions or performance.	performance=expectation x value / Combining the importance or value of a goal and the likelihood of actually getting it or expectation will inform future performance.
A 141	A 142
They believed people wanted to feel like they were successful so they would modify their behaviors to either achieve success or avoid failure. this is known as the need for achievement.	desire success
A 143	A 144
It is the conflict one feels when a particular goal has both positive and negative valence like going on a beach vacation (positive valence) when one's is afraid to fly (negative valence).	pleasure pain

Q 145

Hebb suggested that a moderate amount of _____ is required for motivation and performance.

Q 146

Stopping at red lights is an example of what type of learning?

Q 147

What is the opposite of incidental learning?

Q 148

Decreased response to a familiar stimulus is called what?

Q 149

Experiments in which an animal presses a bar to get a reward are examples of what?

Q 150

What is the term for one strong stimulus preventing conditioning to a weaker stimulus?

Q 151

What is the opposite of habituation?

Q 152

How did M.E. Olds help provide evidence against drive-reduction theory?

A 145 arousal / Too much or too little arousal will prevent optimal performance on a task. This is known as the Yerkes-Dodson effect.	A 146 response learning
A 147 intentional learning / Incidental learning happens accidentally not on purpose.	A 148 habituation
A 149 autoshaping / The animal is changing its own behavior by responding to the reward.	A 150 overshadowing
A 151 sensitization / Instead of decreasing responsiveness to a stimulus one becomes more sensitive to a stimulus after repeated exposure.	A 152 He used electrical stimulation of the brain's pleasure centers as a form of positive reinforcement and showed that animals would alter their behavior to receive the stimulation.

Q 153

Is it easier to learn continuous motor tasks or discrete motor tasks?

Q 154

At what age is it easiest to learn new things? At what age is it the hardest?

Q 155

What is Hermann Ebbinghaus famous for?

Q 156

Who wrote the first psychology textbook and who wrote the first educational psychology textbook?

Q 157

The measure of one's capacity to perform a task or learn something new is called what?

Q 158

What is scaffolding (or scaffolding learning)?

Q 159

What are the three stages of memory?

Q 160

What is the function of sensory memory?

A 153	A 154
continuous tasks / When like riding a bicycle one motor task flows into the next it is easier to learn than a series of individual motor tasks.	People are able to learn new things most easily between the ages of 3 and 20. After age 50 people are least able to learn.

A 155	A 156
his learning curve / He posited that people learn at different rates. Sometimes people learn very quickly early on in a subject or task and then plateau and learn at a slower rate than before.	Wundt in 1874 Thorndike in 1903

A 157	A 158
aptitude	Scaffolding is the process of providing a learner with less and less support as it is needed until no assistance is required.

A 159	A 160
sensory memory / short-term memory / long-term memory	Sensory memory is a buffer between what is in the world and what we actually take into our minds. This information is held for less than a second before it is lost or transferred to short-term memory.

Q 161

What are the common properties of sensory memory?

Q 162

What did George Sperling study?

Q 163

What term did Ulric Neisser coin in the field of visual memory?

Q 164

If you see a picture, then immediately see another one, you will have weakened memory of the first picture. What is this phenomenon called?

Q 165

What is echoic memory?

Q 166

What kind of memory is used when you say a number over and over (rehearsal) before you dial it into your phone?

Q 167

What is the type of rehearsal that allows short-term memories to transfer to long-term memory?

Q 168

To what does George Miller's finding regarding "the magical number seven, plus or minus two" refer?

A 161	A 162
concise duration / connects memory to the perception / includes echoic and iconic memory	iconic memory

A 163	A 164
icon / An icon is a fleeting visual memory that lasts only about half a second.	backward masking / The closer the second stimulus is to the first the better it will "mask" the first. This is also the case when listening to and remembering sounds.

A 165	A 166
Like iconic memory echoic memory holds an exact copy of a sound in our sensory memory for a few seconds.	Short-term memory is used and lasts in your brain for roughly 10-30 seconds. Information in short-term memory is lost due to interference.

A 167	A 168
elaborative rehearsal	This phrase refers to the idea of chunking which states that we can recall roughly seven chunks of information from our short-term memory plus or minus two chunks.

Q 169

Since short-term memory is believed to be more auditory than visual, how are stimuli encoded?

Q 170

What are the types of interference?

Q 171

If your favorite sports team gets newly designed jerseys, you may forget what the old jerseys looked like over time. What kind of interference is occurring?

Q 172

What kind of memory is used when remembering your own phone number?

Q 173

What are the three measures of memory retention?

Q 174

What is recognition?

Q 175

What principle says that you should take a test in the same seat you were in when you learned the material for the test in order to remember it better?

Q 176

What are the three types of long-term memory?

A 169 phonologically	A 170 proactive interference and retroactive interference
A 171 retroactive interference / New information entering your memory clouds the old memories inhibiting their recall.	A 172 Long-term memory which can last for days weeks years or life. Very little gets transferred from your short-term to your long-term memory.
A 173 recall / recognition / savings (or relearning)	A 174 Recognition is the easiest form of memory retention measurement since all it requires is someone remembering that they have been exposed to the stimulus before.
A 175 the encoding specificity principle	A 176 episodic memory / semantic memory / procedural memory

Q 177

What kind of memory is used when riding a bike?

Q 178

What kind of memory is used when remembering a fact?

Q 179

What kind of memory accounts for the fact that you know how to tie your shoes, even though you can't remember when you learned it?

Q 180

If an individual can form new memories but is unable to recall any autobiographical memories from before the onset of amnesia, what kind of amnesia does he have?

Q 181

What is another term for photographic memory?

Q 182

What well-known major contribution did Hermann Ebbinghaus make to the understanding of memory?

Q 183

Explain Ebbinghaus' forgetting curve.

Q 184

What did Brenda Milner contribute to memory research?

A 177	A 178
Procedural memory is the part of long-term memory that remembers how to perform an action.	declarative memory

A 179	A 180
Implicit memories are unconscious and sometimes you don't even know you have those memories.	Retrograde amnesia which prevents the recall of autobiographical memories before the onset of amnesia.

A 181	A 182
eidetic memory	Hermann Ebbinghaus (1850-1909) first established primacy recency and the serial position and forgetting curves?

A 183	A 184
When we learn new information much of it is lost almost immediately after learning it. After this initial drop however forgetting nearly plateaus and the loss of memory is far less drastic.	Mood-congruent memory is the process of recalling memories that match our moods. So if you are sad you will remember other sad memories but if you are happy you will recall other happy memories.

Q 185	Q 186
Who studied memory implantation and found that the memories we make can be altered without our awareness?	What does the levels-of-processing theory suggest?
Q 187	**Q 188**
What rhyme is closely associated with Donald Hebb's theory of learning and memory?	What does the serial position curve illustrate?
Q 189	**Q 190**
What is serial anticipation?	What kind of learning is used during exposure to new vocabulary words in a different language?
Q 191	**Q 192**
free recall	What are some things that help people remember lists?

A 185 Milner studied amnesic patient "HM" who had hippocampal lesions due to epilepsy. HM showed that amnesics could form new implicit memories without forming accompanying explicit memories.	A 186 the levels-of-processing theory
A 187 Memories are not stored in one specific area (though some areas are closely linked with memory) but are distributed to various areas of the cortex.	A 188 He provided experimental support for the theory with his research on the synaptic changes in brains of the Aplysia (sea slug).
A 189 Serial learning is learning lists of items in a specific order like the states in alphabetical order or the chronology of U.S. presidents.	A 190 Serial anticipation is learning a serial list but then recalling the items from the list using the previous correct answer as a cue for the following answer.
A 191 The paired association is used to create a match between something we know and something we don't know like "cheese" in English and "fromage" in French.	A 192 Participants learn items on a list then must recall them without cues or a particular order.

Q 193 What are the two theories of forgetting?	**Q 194** What is the decay (or trace) theory?
Q 195 Why does the interference theory state we lose our memories?	**Q 196** What are memory tricks like "Roy G. Biv" called?
Q 197 When participants are exposed to new information they are not told to remember, they are tested on that information, what is being measured?	**Q 198** According to the generation-recognition model, why is a fill-in-the-blank test more difficult than a multiple choice test?
Q 199 Explain Collins' and Loftus' spreading activation model.	**Q 200** Can hypnosis aid in accurate memory retrieval?

A 193	A 194
importance / brevity / acoustic and semantic dissimilarity / familiarity / concreteness	decay theory (or trace theory) / interference theory

A 195	A 196
Decay theory is the belief that forgetting is caused by memory decay and that memories just naturally fade over time.	Much like it sounds interference theory suggests that other things in the mind get in the way to block memories between learning and recall.

A 197	A 198
mnemonics / Mnemonics are ways to remember things by placing them in an order that is easy to remember like making up a name to remember the colors of the rainbow.	incidental learning

A 199	A 200
Words that are semantically similar are linked together and more likely encoded into long-term memory than words that are acoustically similar or semantically dissimilar because meaning is created.	According to the Zeigarnik effect we remember unfinished tasks better.

Q 201

What type of thinking is used to figure out the solution to a math problem?

Q 202

What type of thinking is used when figuring out alternate sources of energy?

Q 203

What is a term used for the understanding of how things generally go?

Q 204

_____ are the way we represent the connectedness of two or more items or ideas.

Q 205

What is a heuristic? What are its benefits and drawbacks?

Q 206

Describe the James-Lange theory of emotion.

Q 207

What are the two factors of Schachter and Singer's two-factor theory of emotion?

Q 208

Building perception of an object by mentally compiling all of its features is called what?

A 201 convergent thinking / Convergent thinking is used when there is one solution to a particular problem.	A 202 divergent thinking / Divergent thinking is used if there are multiple solutions to a problem or if there is a dissenter to a particular way of thinking.
A 203 scripts / For a birthday party a script might include decorations attendees cake etc.	A 204 Concepts / ex: a coat is an item of clothing with long sleeves that opens in the front and keeps us warm
A 205 A heuristic is a way of solving a problem that uses common sense rules of thumb or educated guesses. It is not always accurate but it is faster than an algorithm.	A 206 This theory asserts that changes in physiological states occur before and result in emotion.
A 207 physiological arousal / how we cognitively label the experience of arousal	A 208 bottom-up processing or feature analysis / This is slower than top-down processing but is more thorough and less prone to mistakes and is data-driven.

Q 209 What is "thinking about thinking" known as?	**Q 210** What are some logical reasoning errors?
Q 211 If your mother accuses you of something and then uses every aspect of your arguments and body language to prove that you did it, what logical reasoning error is she using?	**Q 212** How might the atmosphere effect prevent you from proper reasoning?
Q 213 How is cognitive processing often measured?	**Q 214** Who suggested that people can say two similar items or concepts are related more quickly than they can say two dissimilar items or concepts are unrelated?
Q 215 Why is it that Allan Collins and Ross Quinlan suggest it takes longer to find a link between loosely associated stimuli than closely associated stimuli?	**Q 216** How does semantic priming reduce latency in word-recognition tasks?

A 209	A 210
metacognition	With deductive reasoning information leads to a single conclusion. With inductive reasoning the specificity of information leads to larger more general rules.

A 211	A 212
confirmation bias / semantic effect / atmosphere effect	She is employing confirmation bias which looks for any piece of evidence (even if it's wrong) to confirm a belief or solution to a problem.

A 213	A 214
insight	It is measured by reaction time which is also called latency.

A 215	A 216
Elizabeth Loftus and Allan Collins / They suggest that semantically similar items or concepts are grouped together in memory.	parallel distributive processing or connectionism

Q 217	Q 218
What is the term for processing that is contained within a larger organizational process, thus happening without additional cognitive effort?	How can information processing be measured while a participant is reading?
Q 219	**Q 220**
What are saccades?	How do hypotheses inform our ideas of concepts?
Q 221	**Q 222**
How can a mental set help or hinder the attempt to solve a problem?	In psychology, what are prototypes?
Q 223	**Q 224**
When solving a problem, what is the name given to the entirety of solutions possible?	Who created the "logical theorist" and the "general problem solver" and what did they do?

A 217	A 218
Semantic priming exposes a participant to a particular word without their awareness and is more quickly recalled later because it has been activated in the semantic hierarchy.	automatic processing
A 219	**A 220**
eye movements and gaze durations	movements of the eye between fixation points
A 221	**A 222**
Hypotheses allow us to test our existing ideas of relatedness helping us to form new concepts or strengthen the concepts we already have.	schema / Schemas (or schemata) are formed by existing understandings of how the world works. New information either fits into the existing schema or changes it.
A 223	**A 224**
Prototypes are the most representative characteristics of an item or concept.	problem space

Q 225	Q 226
Though hotly contested, what is a simple definition for intelligence?	What is a base-rate fallacy?

Q 227	Q 228
What are the seven defined intelligences in Howard Gardner's theory of multiple intelligences?	What were the two types of mental abilities Raymond Cattell theorized?

Q 229	Q 230
In our youth, _____ intelligence increases as we learn to solve new problems. As we age, we have more _____ intelligence, stemming from schooling or experience.	What is the difference between sensation and perception?

Q 231	Q 232
What are the three stages of sensation?	Stimuli from the outside world are converted into neural impulses to be processed by our brains through what process?

A 225 Allen Newell and Herbert Simon and they were computer simulation models which were designed to solve problems the way a human would.	A 226 the capacity to perform better in an environment by applying knowledge
A 227 using personal beliefs or stereotypical attitudes instead of numerical data to form a conclusion	A 228 primary mental abilities
A 229 fluid intelligence / crystallized intelligence	A 230 The sensation is what happens when our sensory modalities (vision hearing taste etc.) are activated. / Perception is how we understand these senses.
A 231 reception / transduction / transmission through neural pathways to the brain	A 232 transduction

Q 233

If you are zoning out in class and your teacher suddenly uses a swear word, you will snap back to attention. What is the phenomenon called that is responsible for this?

Q 234

What are the "energy senses" and why are they called that?

Q 235

What are the "chemical senses" and why are they called that?

Q 236

What is a human's dominant sense?

Q 237

cornea

Q 238

pupil

Q 239

iris

Q 240

lens

A 233	A 234
The cocktail party phenomenon/effect involuntarily focuses our attention on something salient like hearing our name in a roomful of people or hearing a teacher curse.	vision / audition (hearing) / touch / These senses convert stimuli into energy like light sound waves and pressure.

A 235	A 236
taste (gustation) / smell (olfaction) / These senses take stimuli and convert them into chemical signals to be processed.	vision

A 237	A 238
The cornea is the protective covering of the eye where light first enters and is focused.	The black part in the middle of the eye the pupil acts like the shutter of a camera and is controlled by the iris.

A 239	A 240
The iris is the colored disc surrounding the pupil that changes its dilation allowing more or less light in.	The lens focuses light entering through the pupil (called accommodation) then flips and inverts the image and projects it onto the retina.

Q 241 retina	Q 242 What are the parts of the retina?
Q 243 When the sun sets and everything in the dark around you looks bluish, are your rods or your cones activated?	Q 244 fovea
Q 245 Why do we have a "blind spot"?	Q 246 The optic nerve is comprised of axons from what?
Q 247 What is the lateral geniculate nucleus (LGN)?	Q 248 After visual impulses are processed in the thalamus, where do they end up?

A 241	A 242
The upside-down and inverted image is projected onto the retina where neurons are activated to interpret the image via transduction. The retina has several layers of cells involved in transduction.	rods and cones / fovea / ganglion cells / blind spot

A 243	A 244
Rods are activated. Rods react to light rather than color with the exception of blue which explains why we can only see shades of blue in the dark. Cones are activated by other colors.	The fovea is an indentation in the retina. It is the eye's fixation point or the part of the eye used when attending to detail.

A 245	A 246
The area where the optic nerve leaves the retina has no photoreceptors (rods or cones).	ganglion cells

A 247	A 248
It is the visual part of the thalamus that receives information from the optic nerve.	Vision is ultimately processed by the occipital lobe.

Q 249	Q 250
There are five feature detectors in vision, labeled V1 through V5. Who won the Nobel Prize for their discovery?	**In the context of vision, what does each of the five feature detectors do?**
Q 251	Q 252
What is trichromatic theory?	**What characteristics of a sound wave determine what we actually hear?**
Q 253	Q 254
pinna	eardrum
Q 255	Q 256
ossicles	oval window

A 249	A 250
David Hubel and Torsten Wiesel	V1. mental image formation and imagination / V2. illusory contours / V3. location / V4. color analysis and pattern recognition / V5. motion and direction
A 251	**A 252**
It is the theory that the cones in our retinas perceive blue green and red and are activated in combination to create a perception of all the colors in the visual spectrum.	The amplitude of a soundwave determines the loudness of a sound (decibels). / The frequency of a soundwave determines the pitch of a sound (hertz).
A 253	**A 254**
The pinna is the flap of skin outside the ear that helps capture and focus sound.	The eardrum or tympanic membrane concentrates sound energy vibrating when sound from the ear canal hits it.
A 255	**A 256**
Ossicles are three tiny bones in the middle ear that connect the eardrum to the oval window. / hammer (malleus) / anvil (incus) / stirrup (stapes)	The oval window compresses the fluid in the cochlea and connects the middle ear to the inner ear.

Q 257 cochlea	Q 258 What is the frequency theory?
Q 259 When you go to a loud concert and stand by the speakers, what kind of deafness are you causing for yourself?	Q 260 What kind of deafness is caused when one of the mechanisms used to move sound from the outer ear to the cochlea is damaged?
Q 261 What sensory modality responds to pressure or temperature?	Q 262 What are papillae?
Q 263 What are the five different tastes we perceive?	Q 264 What is another word for "taste"?

A 257	A 258
The fluid-filled cochlea is small and coiled like a snail's shell and converts vibrational activity into neural energy.	Frequency theory (or volley theory) says that we hear different pitches because of the frequency at which the hair cells in the cochlea fire.
A 259	**A 260**
nerve deafness / Loud noises damage the hair cells on the cochlea preventing them from firing for any sounds at all so no neural impulses reach the brain.	conduction deafness
A 261	**A 262**
touch	Papillae are the bumps on your tongue that hold taste buds.
A 263	**A 264**
salty / sweet / bitter / sour / umami (savory or meaty tastes)	gestation

Q 265

What makes a smell different from the other senses? Why do certain smells trigger memories?

Q 266

What is the kinesthetic sense in charge of?

Q 267

What is the absolute threshold?

Q 268

If your parents ask you to turn down the television, what determines how much you have to turn it down before they notice a change in volume?

Q 269

What theory takes into account the things that distract us from perceiving a stimulus?

Q 270

What is top-down processing?

Q 271

Building perception of an object by mentally compiling all of its features is called what?

Q 272

What are the four Gestalt rules of perception?

A 265	A 266
It is not processed through the thalamus. Instead the nerves of the olfactory bulb connect with the amygdala and hippocampus which are attached to memory and emotional response.	The kinesthetic sense keeps track of specific body parts and where they are in space using receptors in joints and muscles.
A 267	A 268
It is the smallest stimulus consciously perceptible at least 50% of the times encountered. Stimuli below the absolute threshold are considered subliminal.	The difference threshold (or just-noticeable difference) is the amount a stimulus needs to change before the change can be detected. For hearing the change must be 5%.
A 269	A 270
Signal detection theory acknowledges the motivation to perceive a certain stimulus like smelling delicious food when we're hungry or not noticing a friend in a crowded room.	Top-down processing uses the information we already have in our brains to fill in gaps in the things we sense. It can frequently overrule the more primitive areas of our brains.
A 271	A 272
bottom-up processing or feature analysis / This is slower than top-down processing but is more thorough and less prone to mistakes.	proximity / continuity / similarity / closure

Q 273	Q 274
proximity	continuity

Q 275	Q 276
similarity	closure

Q 277	Q 278
While objects frequently remain the same, the way we view them does not. What allows us to still recognize an item despite the changes in how we see it?	What prevents us from thinking an object is actually changing in size as we walk toward it?

Q 279	Q 280
_____ allows us to know that the color of an object does not change, even though the light hitting it does change.	_____ are used to perceive depth, and require use of both eyes, while _____ only require use of one eye.

A 273	A 274
Items close together are easy to perceive as being part of the same group.	Items that form a continuous pattern are easier for the mind to see as part of the same group.

A 275	A 276
Items that look alike are more likely to be seen as being in the same group.	Items that form a known image are easier to group together even if there are some gaps within the image.

A 277	A 278
Constancy allows this to happen. There are three types of constancy: / size constancy / shape constancy / brightness (or color) constancy	Size constancy helps take distance into account when calculating the size of an object.

A 279	A 280
Brightness constancy (or color constancy)	Binocular cues monocular cues

Q 281	Q 282
What are examples of monocular cues?	linear perspective
Q 283	Q 284
relative size cues	interposition cues
Q 285	Q 286
texture gradient	shadowing
Q 287	Q 288
What are two binocular cues to help us perceive depth?	How does convergence signal how far away an object is?

A 281 linear perspective / relative size cues / interposition cues / texture gradient / shadowing	A 282 Like in art class linear perspective uses a point on the canvas for two lines to come together representing distance.
A 283 To represent distance objects in photos or drawings tend to be larger the closer they are to the foreground. If something is in the distance it is usually represented as being quite small.	A 284 Interposition cues signal to a viewer that an object obscuring the view of another object is closer to the viewer.
A 285 Things in the distance are difficult to see clearly and things close-up are more detailed so fuzzy textures signal that an object or landscape is in the distance.	A 286 Shadowing uses light and darkness to signal to the viewer the location of objects.
A 287 binocular disparity (or retinal disparity) / convergence	A 288 The muscles that control the eyes send signals to the brain as they move and the more the eye muscles converge (turn inward together) the closer an object must be.

Q 289 **What muscles control the shape of the lens?**	Q 290 **Rods and cones are also known as what?**
Q 291 **In what part of the retina is visual acuity at its greatest?**	Q 292 **How would nativists explain perception?**
Q 293 **How would structuralists explain perception?**	Q 294 **How would gestalt psychologists explain perception?**
Q 295 **What are people with prosopagnosia unable to do?**	Q 296 **Why does a single light in darkness appear to move?**

A 289	A 290
ciliary muscles	receptor cells

A 291	A 292
The fovea since it has the greatest concentration of cones in the eye enabling the perception of fine detail.	Nativists would argue that perception is innate.

A 293	A 294
Structuralists would argue that perception is a result of bottom-up processing stemming from sensory input.	They would argue that perception is a result of top-down processing since the way people explain the world is by creating a system of organization.

A 295	A 296
recognize faces / Prosopagnosia appears to affect the fusiform gyrus and can be either following brain trauma or congenital.	The constant motion of our own eyes causes static objects to appear in motion which is referred to as the autokinetic effect.

Q 297

What does the basilar membrane do?

Q 298

What type of cells responds to pain and temperature changes in the skin?

Q 299

What do Pacinian corpuscles respond to?

Q 300

What are the fast-adapting skin receptor cells that respond to light touch?

Q 301

What is the two-point threshold?

Q 302

When you feel neither warm nor cold, your skin may be experiencing what?

Q 303

Mirror boxes have been shown to reduce what?

Q 304

What causes us to turn in the direction of something touching us?

A 297 The basilar membrane vibrates in response to sound coming from the stapes.	A 298 free nerve endings
A 299 vibration	A 300 Meissner's corpuscles
A 301 It is the point at which touch from two separate objects is recognized. Different places on the body have smaller or larger two-point thresholds.	A 302 physiological zero / Usually around 85 degrees Fahrenheit this is the point at which your skin will not feel temperature sensations.
A 303 phantom limb pain / Phantom limb pain is when an amputee feels pain in the limb that is no longer attached.	A 304 the orienting reflex

Q 305 **Who defined the just-noticeable difference (or differential threshold)?**	Q 306 **What is the visual field?**
Q 307 **What causes us to understand that a train is in the distance because it appears to be moving slowly and a train is close because it appears to be moving quickly?**	Q 308 **What causes perceived differences in brightness in visual regions?**
Q 309 **Who suggested the tri-color theory (or component theory)?**	Q 310 **What neuronal layers stand between the rods and cones and the optic nerve?**
Q 311 **What are the three types of cells Hubel and Wiesel differentiated with regard to signal detection theory?**	Q 312 **What photopigment is contained in the rods?**

A 305 E. H. Weber	A 306 The visual field is the total perceptible area at any given time without moving your head or eyes.
A 307 the motion parallax	A 308 lateral inhibition / Interconnected neurons inhibit each other to produce contrast at the edges of regions.
A 309 Thomas Young and Hermann von Helmholtz / Helmholtz is also known for his theory on color blindness.	A 310 horizontal cells / amacrine cells / bipolar cells / ganglion cells
A 311 simple: concerned with boundaries and orientation of an object / complex: information about the movement / hypercomplex: information about the shape	A 312 rhodopsin

Q 313

The law of prä,gnanz allows us to find complex and specific details in objects.

Q 314

What type of motion occurs when a stationary point of light has the appearance of the movement against a moving background?

Q 315

The motion aftereffect states that if we see an object in motion for a long time and then it stops, it will appear to move in the _____ direction even though it is not moving at all.

Q 316

What brain structures are important for visual processing?

Q 317

What brain structures are important for auditory processing?

Q 318

What brain structure is important for processing touch?

Q 319

What is neuroanatomy?

Q 320

What is a neuron?

A 313 false / The law of prägnanz says we organize the things we perceive in the simplest or most orderly way possible.	A 314 induced motion
A 315 opposite	A 316 lateral genigulate nucleus (thalamus) / superior colliculus / visual cortex (occipital lobe)
A 317 inferior colliculus / medial geniculate nucleus (thalamus) / auditory cortex (temporal lobe)	A 318 somatosensory cortex
A 319 Neuroanatomy relates to the parts and functions of individual nerve cells known as neurons.	A 320 A neuron is an individual nerve cell.

Q 321	Q 322
Name the parts of a neuron.	dendrite
Q 323	**Q 324**
cell body/soma	axon hillock
Q 325	**Q 326**
axon	terminal buttons
Q 327	**Q 328**
What are synonyms for "terminal buttons"?	Chemicals travel within the cells but are transmitted to other neurons electrically.

A 321	A 322
dendrites / cell body/soma / axon hillock / axon / myelin sheath / nodes of Ranvier / terminal buttons / neurotransmitters / synapse/synaptic cleft	Dendrites are branch-like arms attached to the cell body that receive information from other neurons.

A 323	A 324
The cell body/soma is the "brain" of the neuron making up the gray matter and containing the nucleus.	connects the cell body to the axon

A 325	A 326
Axons are tube-like structures that transmit information (via electrical impulse) from the cell body to the terminal buttons.	Terminal buttons are where information from the axon ends up and contain neurotransmitters.

A 327	A 328
end buttons / synaptic knobs / axon terminals / terminal branches of axons	false / Within the cells information is transmitted as an electric signal but when it reaches the axon terminal it is converted into chemicals that move between one neuron and the next.

Q 329 **Can a neuron fire at different magnitudes?**	Q 330 Some _____ are excitatory, prodding the cell body to fire, and others are _____, which prevent the creation of a cell's action potential.
Q 331 **Describe the path of information within a neuron from beginning to end.**	Q 332 **When neurotransmitters from the axon terminal are released, they attempt to connect with _____ on the postsynaptic dendrite.**
Q 333 threshold	Q 334 acetylcholine
Q 335 endorphins	Q 336 serotonin

A 329	A 330
No a neuron will fire completely if it reaches or exceeds the depolarization threshold or not at all which is called the all-or-none principle.	neurotransmitters inhibitory

A 331	A 332
Dendrite (chemical signals)⇒cell body (become electrical signals)⇒axon⇒axon terminal (become chemical signals)⇒synapse⇒dendrite of next neuron	receptor sites

A 333	A 334
The threshold is the level of depolarization a cell body must reach to produce an action potential.	Function: motor movement / Problem: Alzheimer's disease linked to acetylcholine deficit

A 335	A 336
Function: pleasure and pain control / Problem: endorphins are released when pleasure areas of the brain are stimulated so addictions are linked to endorphins	Function: mood control / Problem: deficiency linked to clinical depression / Serotonin is a monoamine and part of the indolamine class.

Q 337 **What is the difference between afferent and efferent neurons?**	Q 338 **What are the subdivisions of the nervous system?**
Q 339 **What is the difference between the central nervous system and the peripheral nervous system?**	Q 340 **When you want to answer a question in class, what part of the nervous system controls your ability to raise your hand?**
Q 341 **When did your stomach begin to growl before lunch, what part of the nervous system is activated?**	Q 342 **What are the ways in which psychologists study the functions of different brain areas?**
Q 343 **electroencephalogram (EEG)**	Q 344 **Computerized Axial Tomography**

A 337 Afferent neurons or sensory neurons carry information to the brain. / Efferent neurons or motor neurons carry information from the brain to the body.	A 338 central nervous system / brain and spinal cord / peripheral nervous system / somatic / autonomic / sympathetic / parasympathetic
A 339 The central nervous system includes the nerves in bones. The peripheral nervous system includes the nerves not encased in bone.	A 340 The somatic nervous system controls voluntary muscle movements.
A 341 The autonomic nervous system is activated which controls the parts of our bodies that work automatically like heartbeats breathing and digestive muscles.	A 342 accidents / lesions / electroencephalogram (EEG) / Computerized Axial Tomography (CAT or CT) / Magnetic Resonance Imaging (MRI) / Positron Emission Tomography (PET) / Functional MRI (fMRI)
A 343 Used largely in sleep research the electroencephalogram (EEG) detects brain waves during different states of consciousness.	A 344 Also known as a CAT or CT this method can get a three-dimensional X-ray image of the brain which is helpful for detecting structural problems like tumors but does not aid in detecting brain activity.

Q 345 **Positron Emission Tomography**	Q 346 **What parts of the brain are located in the hindbrain?**
Q 347 pons	Q 348 reticular formation
Q 349 **Where are the thalamus, hypothalamus, amygdala, and hippocampus located in the brain?**	Q 350 **What are the parts of the brain known as the limbic system, and what function does the limbic system serve?**
Q 351 thalamus	Q 352 hypothalamus

A 345	A 346
The PET allows psychologists to see activity in the brain by monitoring how much of a chemical different parts of the brain are using.	myelencephalon (medulla) / metencephalon (pons and cerebellum) / the base of the reticular formation
A 347	**A 348**
The pons connects the forebrain midbrain and hindbrain and helps control facial expression.	Located in the midbrain the reticular formation controls bodily arousal and our ability to focus. / The reticular formation is believed to be the oldest part of the brain.
A 349	**A 350**
the forebrain	thalamus / hypothalamus / hippocampus / amygdala / septal area / The limbic system is involved in "fight flight feeding and fornication."
A 351	**A 352**
Known as the "sensory way station" of the brain the thalamus receives information from the spinal cord and routes it to the appropriate part of the forebrain for further processing.	The hypothalamus controls the endocrine system as well as metabolic functions like libido body temperature hunger and thirst.

Q 353 hippocampus	Q 354 amygdala
Q 355 Why are our brains wrinkled?	Q 356 If you want to kick a soccer ball with your right foot, which hemisphere of the brain controls this, and what principle explains it?
Q 357 Split-brain patients have had their _____ severed, usually to treat epilepsy. What two doctors pioneered this surgical procedure?	Q 358 corpus callosum
Q 359 There are four lobes in the brain. Name them.	Q 360 What area of the brain allows us to move our muscles to produce speech?

A 353	A 354
The hippocampus is responsible for converting short-term memories to long-term memories.	The amygdala controls emotion and fear.
A 355	**A 356**
The surface of the brain is covered with neurons and wrinkles (or fissures) increase the surface area so more neurons can connect with one another to transmit more information.	The left hemisphere controls the motor function on the right half of the body and vice versa. This is called contralateral control.
A 357	**A 358**
corpus callosum / Roger Sperry and Michael Gazzaniga pioneered this procedure.	The corpus callosum is the nerve bundle that runs through the middle of the brain connecting the hemispheres.
A 359	**A 360**
frontal / parietal / occipital / temporal	Broca's area which is located in the left frontal lobe in most right-handers

Q 361

The top of the motor cortex controls voluntary muscle movements in what area of the body?

Q 362

Located in the parietal lobe behind the motor cortex, the _____ receives touch sensations from the body.

Q 363

Damage to what area of the temporal lobe would result in an inability to understand written or spoken language?

Q 364

What sensory modality is the temporal lobe responsible for the processing?

Q 365

nodes of Ranvier

Q 366

What are the parts of the mesencephalon (midbrain)?

Q 367

What is the purpose of the rectum?

Q 368

What is the purpose of the tegmentum?

A 361	A 362
The feet and toes are controlled by the top of the motor cortex located at the back of the frontal lobe. The top of the body is controlled by the bottom of the motor cortex.	sensory cortex or somatosensory cortex

A 363	A 364
Wernicke's area	hearing/audition / Unlike vision hearing is not lateralized. The sound coming in one ear is processed by both hemispheres of the brain.

A 365	A 366
the gap between adjacent myelinated segments on the axon	The midbrain contains the tectum and the tegmentum.

A 367	A 368
The tectum which includes the inferior and superior colliculi controls vision and audition.	The tegmentum is home to the remainder of the reticular formation and helps control the sensorimotor system.

Q 369

What does gray matter consist of?

Q 370

What makes up white matter in the brain?

Q 371

What are the divisions of the forebrain?

Q 372

The posterior part of the forebrain, the diencephalon, contains what two brain parts?

Q 373

The frontal portion of the forebrain, the telencephalon, contains what parts of the brain?

Q 374

The corticospinal tract, also known as the pyramidal tract, connects what?

Q 375

What does the pituitary gland do?

Q 376

What part of the brain is implicated in the direction of attention and emotion?

A 369	A 370
cell bodies and dendrites	myelin sheathing / axon bundles / nerve fibers

A 371	A 372
diencephalon / telencephalon	the thalamus and the hypothalamus

A 373	A 374
the limbic system / hippocampus / amygdala / cingulate gyrus	the brain and the spine

A 375	A 376
controls the other glands within the hormonal and endocrine systems	the cingulate gyrus

Q 377	Q 378
What do the superior colliculi control?	What do the inferior colliculi do?
Q 379	**Q 380**
What do the dura mater, pia mater, and arachnoid make up and what do they do?	How does the blood-brain barrier help protect the brain from toxic intruders?
Q 381	Q 382
What are ventricles?	What do the basal ganglia include?
Q 383	Q 384
What is the function of the basal ganglia, and what can happen when they are not working properly?	What are the parts of the cerebral cortex?

A 377	A 378
the direction of visual gaze and direction of visual attention to stimuli	receive auditory information
A 379	**A 380**
These three sheets of tissue comprise the meninges which surround and protect the brain and spinal cord.	The blood-brain barrier is a tightly-formed group of endothelial cells in blood vessels that makes it difficult for larger potentially toxic molecules within the bloodstream to enter the brain.
A 381	**A 382**
fluid-filled cavities that prevent the brain from shock by acting as a cushion	caudate nucleus / putamen / globus pallidus / substantia nigra
A 383	**A 384**
The basal ganglia help control motor function so improper functioning can be linked to Parkinson's and Huntington's diseases.	frontal lobe / parietal lobe / occipital lobe / temporal lobe / neocortex / gyri and sulci

Q 385 **How many layers does the neocortex have?**	Q 386 **What are the bumps and ridges in the brain called?**
Q 387 **What are the parts of the brain called that are linked with certain responses to stimuli?**	Q 388 **apraxia**
Q 389 **agnosia**	Q 390 **aphasia**
Q 391 **alexia**	Q 392 **agraphia**

A 385	A 386
six	bumps are gyri (singular: gyrus) and furrows or fissures are sulci (singular: sulcus)
A 387	**A 388**
cortical association areas	impairment in the ability to start and organize voluntary movements (no muscle paralysis involved)
A 389	**A 390**
difficulty in recognition of objects	impairment in the language (can be impaired understanding or production)
A 391	**A 392**
inability to read	inability to write

Q 393 What is the result of Broca's aphasia?	Q 394 Damage to Wernicke's area creates what deficiency?
Q 395 hyperphagia	Q 396 Following damage to or removal of the cerebral cortex, what behavioral side effect might occur?
Q 397 What type of tools are used to implant electrodes in the brains of animals?	Q 398 What floral term is used to describe the beginnings of plasticity in children?
Q 399 What holds neurotransmitters as they are transported to the synaptic cleft?	Q 400 In order for an action potential to occur, ions must permeate what?

A 393	A 394
When a person has damage to Broca's area he is able to understand language but language production is impaired.	Wernicke's aphasia is marked by impaired language comprehension from others and production of fluent but meaningless speech.
A 395	A 396
excessive overeating linked with damage to the ventromedial hypothalamus	decorticate rage (or sham rage) which is intense but not clearly directed rage
A 397	A 398
stereotaxic instruments	"Blooming and pruning" is the process of growing new neural connections and allowing others to die as young brains learn what is most important for their survival.
A 399	A 400
synaptic vesicles (or synaptic vessels)	the cell membrane

Q 401

What is the function of glial cells?

Q 402

What are the four types of glial cells?

Q 403

_____ form myelin in the central nervous system, while _____ form myelin in the peripheral nervous system.

Q 404

What is the point in transduction when the neuron is negatively charged and an action potential has not yet occurred?

Q 405

What allows the postsynaptic cell's ion channels to open?

Q 406

What are the types of postsynaptic potentials?

Q 407

What is saltatory conduction?

Q 408

After an action potential, a cell is unable to create another action potential during the _____. It will then enter the _____, where it will respond only to strong stimuli.

A 401	A 402
Glial cells are supporting cells providing nutrition materials and chemical signals to neurons in the brain.	Schwann cells / oligodendrocytes / astrocytes / microglia
A 403	A 404
oligodendrocytes Schwann cells	resting potential
A 405	A 406
postsynaptic receptors must recognize the presence of neurotransmitters	excitatory postsynaptic potentials (EPSPs) / inhibitory postsynaptic potentials (IPSPs)
A 407	A 408
Characteristic of myelinated axons saltatory conduction is when an action potential jumps from one node of Ranvier to the next.	absolute refractory period relative refractory period

Q 409

What are the two most important amino acids in the brain?

Q 410

What is the function of glutamate?

Q 411

What is the function of Gamma-aminobutyric acid (GABA)?

Q 412

What do agonists do?

Q 413

What do antagonists do?

Q 414

A fetus will develop into a male if the _____ is present.

Q 415

During puberty, males release _____and females release _____ to cause genital maturation and development of secondary sex characteristics.

Q 416

What is the beginning of the menstrual cycle, occurring during puberty, referred to as?

A 409	A 410
glutamate and gamma-aminobutyric acid (GABA)	Glutamate activates neurons but can become neurotoxic in excess causing neurons to fire too quickly. / Glutamate is the most common excitatory neurotransmitter.

A 411	A 412
GABA is an inhibitory neurotransmitter which helps balance out glutamate and allows the brain to achieve stasis. / It is the most common inhibitory neurotransmitter.	Agonists act like neurotransmitters binding to receptor cells increasing that neurotransmitter's effect. / Xanax is a GABA agonist

A 413	A 414
Antagonists prevent the action of a neurotransmitter decreasing its effect. / Botox is an acetylcholine antagonist	H-Y antigen

A 415	A 416
androgens estrogen	menarche

Q 417 The menstrual cycle is moderated by changes in which hormone levels?	**Q 418** How do the effects of luteinizing hormone (LH) and follicle stimulating hormone (FSH) differ in males and females?
Q 419 What are the principal effects of oxytocin?	**Q 420** What are the principal effects of vasopressin?
Q 421 What signals the thyroid to release hormones?	**Q 422** What does the adrenocorticotropic hormone (ACTH) do?
Q 423 What method is used to study sleep states and patterns?	**Q 424** What are the two main categories of sleep?

A 417	A 418
estradiol / progesterone / luteinizing hormone (LH) / follicle stimulating hormone (FSH)	In females LH and FSH govern ovulation / In males LH and FSH govern sperm and testosterone production
A 419	A 420
Oxytocin stimulates the contraction of uterine muscles during childbirth and the release of breast milk. / Oxytocin is also linked to pair bonding.	Vasopressin stimulates water reabsorption by the kidneys and blood vessel constriction which helps regulate blood pressure.
A 421	A 422
thyroid-stimulating hormone	controls the release of glucocorticoids mineralocorticoids and sex hormones
A 423	A 424
electroencephalography (EEG)	REM (rapid eye movement) and non-REM (or slow-wave sleep)

Q 425 **How long does it take to get through non-REM sleep?**	Q 426 **Describe stage 0 sleep.**
Q 427 **Describe stage 1 sleep.**	Q 428 **Describe stage 2 sleep.**
Q 429 **What are sleep spindles?**	Q 430 **What are K complexes?**
Q 431 **Describe stage 4 sleep.**	Q 432 **Who gets more REM sleep: someone who gets plenty of sleep each night or sleep-deprived graduate students?**

A 425 roughly 90 minutes	A 426 This stage occurs before sleep when relaxing and closing the eyes and is characterized by frequently occurring alpha waves at low levels.
A 427 heart rate slowed muscle tension reduced irregular frequency of EEG waves eyes roll decreased response to stimuli theta waves occur	A 428 heart rate body temperature and respiration decline sleep spindles and K complexes are present in EEG
A 429 Sleep spindles are bursts of high-frequency brain waves during stage 2 sleep.	A 430 Occurring during stage 2 sleep K complexes are sharp drops in EEG potential.
A 431 delta waves are present at least half of the time sleep is the deepest growth hormones are secreted and if woken up one would be extremely groggy	A 432 Those who are sleep-deprived spend more time in REM sleep.

Q 433 **What are interneurons?**	Q 434 **What allows reflexes to occur quickly instead of having to be routed through the brain?**
Q 435 **phylogeny**	Q 436 **What are the subdivisions of the hypothalamus?**
Q 437 **The hypothalamus uses _____ to regulate the balance of water in the body, a process known as _____.**	Q 438 **What is the function of the lateral hypothalamus?**
Q 439 **What is the function of the ventromedial hypothalamus (VMH)?**	Q 440 **What is the function of the anterior hypothalamus?**

A 433	A 434
They are the neurons between other neurons and are linked with reflexes which are imperative for survival.	neural networks known as reflex arcs.
A 435	A 436
the study of evolutionary development	lateral hypothalamus / ventromedial hypothalamus / anterior hypothalamus
A 437	A 438
osmoreceptors osmoregulation	it controls hunger lesions can result in aphagia or a refusal to eat
A 439	A 440
The VMH tells us when we have had enough to eat. Lesions in the VMH can lead to hyperphagia or uncontrollable eating since there is nothing to signal satiety.	It controls sexual behavior. Lesions can lead to inhibited sexual urges and activity.

Q 441

Along with the nucleus accumbens, the _____ is a major pleasure center of the brain.

Q 442

What is Klü,ver-Bucy syndrome?

Q 443

What is another name for the visual cortex?

Q 444

When the sensations from one side of the body communicate with the same side of the cortex, they are communicating _____.

Q 445

What are the three most abundant catecholamines in the body?

Q 446

What two mood disorders are linked to norepinephrine imbalance?

Q 447

What is the synthetic form of dopamine sometimes used to treat patients with Parkinson's disease?

Q 448

Antidepressants like Prozac are called what?

A 441	A 442
septal area (or septum)	It is a syndrome resulting from bilateral lesions to the amygdala marked by docility hypersexuality hyperphagia and hyperorality.
A 443	**A 444**
the striate cortex	ipsilaterally
A 445	**A 446**
dopamine / epinephrine / norepinephrine / They are also classified as monoamines and play a part in emotional processes.	depression and mania
A 447	**A 448**
L-dopa	selective serotonin reuptake inhibitors (SSRIs)

Q 449 **What is the monoamine theory of depression?**	Q 450 **What are peptides?**
Q 451 **What behaviors are associated with epinephrine?**	Q 452 **What are the functions of serotonin?**
Q 453 **What are other terms for sedative-hypnotic drug?**	Q 454 **What are some examples of sedative-hypnotic drugs, and what neurotransmitter do they affect?**
Q 455 **What is Korsakoff's Syndrome?**	Q 456 **What are behavioral stimulants?**

A 449	A 450
This theory believes that excessive or insufficient levels of monoamines (specifical norepinephrine) are linked with mania and depression.	When two or more amino acids combine they form peptides. / Important peptides to remember are endorphins (which serve as natural painkillers) and enkephalins.
A 451	A 452
Epinephrine (or adrenaline) is linked to the fight or flight response.	Serotonin helps regulate mood and eating as well as sleep and dreaming.
A 453	A 454
depressants	alcohol benzodiazepines (like Valium) and barbiturates they enhance GABA and are used as tranquilizers or sedatives.
A 455	A 456
Stemming from malnutrition in chronic alcoholics Korsakoff's syndrome causes anterograde amnesia.	They are drugs that reduce fatigue or increase motor functioning and are believed to increase receptors for the monoamines (dopamine epinephrine norepinephrine) and serotonin.

Q 457

What are some examples of behavioral stimulants, and what are they used for?

Q 458

What are the three main types of antidepressants?

Q 459

How do tricyclic antidepressants work?

Q 460

How do monoamine oxidase (MAO) inhibitors work?

Q 461

What is the purpose of antipsychotic drugs?

Q 462

What are some disorders that can be treated with antipsychotics?

Q 463

What antipsychotic is used frequently to treat bipolar disorder?

Q 464

What are common narcotics (or opiates) and what do they do?

A 457	A 458
amphetamines: used for narcolepsy / antidepressants: used to improve sleep patterns increase activity and elevate mood / methylphenidate (Ritalin): used to treat attention deficit disorder	tricyclics / monoamine oxidase (MAO) inhibitors / selective serotonin reuptake inhibitors (SSRIs)
A 459	A 460
they prevent the reuptake of norepinephrine and serotonin	they prevent MAO from breaking down norepinephrine and serotonin
A 461	A 462
Generally they are believed to prevent dopamine from binding to the postsynaptic membrane reducing hallucinations agitation and delusions.	schizophrenia / bipolar disorder / delusional disorder / psychotic depression / Tourette's syndrome / dementia in the elderly
A 463	A 464
lithium	opium heroin and morphine they are natural painkillers

Q 465	Q 466
What is ablation?	What is dementia?

Q 467	Q 468
scientific method	Define theory as it relates to research methods.

Q 469	Q 470
What is hindsight bias?	What is a controlled experiment?

Q 471	Q 472
hypothesis	How do researchers specifically define what variables mean?

A 465	A 466
Ablation (or extirpation) is the term for surgically induced brain lesions.	a loss of cognitive functioning (including disorientation and memory failure)
A 467	A 468
general procedures psychologists use for gathering and interpreting data	organized testable explanation of phenomena
A 469	A 470
explaining why something happened after it has occurred	researchers systematically manipulate a variable and observe the response in a laboratory
A 471	A 472
prediction of how two or more factors are related	Researchers use operational definitions to precisely describe variables in relation to their study. For example "effectiveness of studying" can be operationally defined with a test score.

Q 473 **What is the difference between an independent variable and a dependent variable in an experiment?**	Q 474 **Define the population as it relates to research methods.**
Q 475 **Define sample as it relates to research methods.**	Q 476 **What type of sample should be used in research?**
Q 477 **The amount of difference between the sample and population is called _____.**	Q 478 **Define random selection as it relates to research methods.**
Q 479 **Which individuals are in the experimental group?**	Q 480 **Which individuals are in the control group?**

A 473	A 474
The factor being manipulated is the independent variable. The factor being measured is the dependent variable.	all the individuals to which the study applies

A 475	A 476
a subgroup of a population that constitutes participants of a study	Larger sample sizes are ideal because they are the most representative of the population.

A 477	A 478
sampling error	every individual from a population has an equal chance of being chosen for the sample

A 479	A 480
subjects who receive the treatment or manipulation of the independent variable	subjects who do not receive any treatment or manipulation

Q 481

Subjects who receive the treatment are part of the _____, while those who do not receive the treatment belong to the _____.

Q 482

What type of experimental design uses experimental and control groups?

Q 483

List four types of confounding variables.

Q 484

Define experimenter bias as it relates to confounding variables.

Q 485

Define demand characteristics as they relate to confounding variables.

Q 486

Define the placebo effect as it relates to confounding variables.

Q 487

What is the Hawthorne effect?

Q 488

What type of experimental design uses each participant as his/her own control?

A 481	A 482
experimental group control group	A between-subjects design uses an experimental group and a control group to compare the effect of the independent variable.
A 483	A 484
experimenter bias / demand characteristics / placebo effect / lack of counterbalancing	Experimenter bias occurs when a researcher's expectations or preferences about the results of the study influence the experiment.
A 485	A 486
clues the participants discover about the intention of the study that alters their responses	responding to an inactive drug with a change in behavior because the subject believes it contains the active ingredient
A 487	A 488
individuals who are being experimented on behaving differently than in their everyday life	A within-subjects design exposes each participant to the treatment and compares their pre-test and post-test results. This design can also compare the results of two different treatments administered.

Q 489	Q 490
What is a single-blind procedure?	**What is a double-blind procedure?**

Q 491	Q 492
Single-blind procedures aim to eliminate the effects of _____, while double-blind procedures use a third party researcher to omit the effects of _____.	**How are quasi-experiments different from controlled experiments?**

Q 493	Q 494
What types of research are considered quasi-experiments?	**correlational research**

Q 495	Q 496
List three methods of data collection	**Define naturalistic observation as it relates to correlational research.**

A 489	A 490
research design in which the subjects are unaware if they are in the control or experimental group	research design in which neither the experimenter nor the subjects are aware of who is in the control or experimental group
A 491	A 492
demand characteristics experimenter bias	Random assignment is not possible in quasi-experiments.
A 493	A 494
Differences in behavior between: / males and females / various age groups / students in different classes	establishes a relationship between two variables / does not determine cause and effect / used to make predictions and generate future research
A 495	A 496
naturalistic observation / surveys / tests	Naturalistic observation consists of field observation of naturally occurring behavior such as the way students behave in the classroom. There is no manipulation of variables.

Q 497 **Define tests as they relate to correlational research.**	Q 498 **_____ studies start by looking at an effect and then attempt to determine the cause.**
Q 499 **What is a case study?**	Q 500 **experiments**
Q 501 **statistics**	Q 502 **What are the four scales of measurement?**
Q 503 **ordinal scale**	Q 504 **interval scale**

A 497 the research method that measures individual traits at a specific time and place	A 498 Ex post facto
A 499 detailed examination of one person or a small group / beneficial for understanding rare and complex phenomena in clinical research / not always representative of the larger population	A 500 Strengths: / determine the cause and effect relationship between variables / control over confounding variables / Weaknesses: / no real-world generalizability / expensive / time-consuming
A 501 analysis of numerical data regarding representative samples	A 502 nominal / ordinal / interval / ratio
A 503 numbers are used as ranks / Examples: / The runner who wins the race is scored as 1 the runner who comes in second is scored as 2 the third is scored as 3 and so on.	A 504 numbers that have a meaningful difference between them / Example: / Temperature: The difference between 10°F and 20°F is the same as between 30°F and 40°F.

Q 505	Q 506
Would the temperature of Celcius and Fahrenheit be measured on an interval scale or a ratio scale?	**What are the descriptive statistics?**

Q 507	Q 508
frequency distribution	**What is the difference between a histogram and a frequency polygon?**

Q 509	Q 510
central tendency	**mode**

Q 511	Q 512
median	**mean**

A 505	A 506
interval / If the temperature is 0°F there is "no temperature." There is not a meaningful ratio between values. 100°F is not twice as hot as 50°F.	numbers that summarize a set of research data from a sample

A 507	A 508
an orderly arrangement of scores indicating the frequency of each score	A histogram is a bar graph and a frequency polygon is a line graph or a bell curve.

A 509	A 510
Measures of central tendency describe the most typical scores for a set of research data. / mode / median / mean	most frequently occurring score in the data set

A 511	A 512
the middle score when the data is ordered by size	the arithmetic average of the scores in the data set

Q 513	Q 514
If two scores appear most frequently, the distribution is _____, and if there are three or more appearing most frequently, it is _____.	When most of the scores are compacted on one side of the bell curve, the distribution is said to be _____.
Q 515	**Q 516**
measures of variability	range
Q 517	**Q 518**
What do the variance and standard deviation measure?	What is a z score (a.k.a. standard score)?
Q 519	**Q 520**
percentile score	What is the term for the line on a scatterplot that follows the trend of the points?

A 513 bimodal multimodal	A 514 skewed / Positively skewed distributions include a lot of small values and negatively skewed distributions include a lot of large values.
A 515 Measures of variability describe the dispersion of scores for a set of research data. / range / variance / standard deviation	A 516 difference between the largest score and the smallest score
A 517 the average difference between each score and the mean of the data set / Taller narrow curves have less variance than short wider curves.	A 518 allows for comparison between different scales / subtract mean from each score and divide by the standard deviation / mean has a z score of zero
A 519 percentage of scores at or below a particular score between 1 and 99 / Example: / If you are in the 70th percentile 70% of the scores are the same as or below yours.	A 520 line of best fit or regression line

Q 521

What is the difference between a null and an alternative hypothesis?

Q 522

What is the difference between a Type I and Type II error?

Q 523

When is a finding statistically significant?

Q 524

What method statistically combines the results of several research studies to reach a conclusion?

Q 525

_____ psychology is practical and designed for real world application, while _____ psychology is focused on research of fundamental principles and theories.

Q 526

Who founded the first psychology research lab?

Q 527

_____ was one of the first psychologists to demonstrate that one could study psychological processes using experimental psychology.

Q 528

Who was the first psychologist to introduce mental testing to the United States?

A 521 Null hypotheses state that treatment had no effect while alternative hypotheses state the treatment did have an effect in the experiment.	A 522 Type I errors or false positives occur if the researcher rejects a true null hypothesis. Type II errors or false negatives occur if the researcher fails to reject a false null hypothesis.
A 523 In psychology a finding is considered statistically significant if the probability (alpha) that the finding is due to chance is less than 1 in 20 (p is less than or equal to 0.05)	A 524 meta-analysis
A 525 Applied basic	A 526 Wilhelm Wundt
A 527 Hermann Ebbinghaus	A 528 James McKeen Cattell

Q 529 Who created the first intelligence test and what was its initial purpose?	Q 530 _____ was a term developed by William Stern, which describes the ratio between someone's chronological and his/her mental age.
Q 531 Who authored the Stanford-Binet Intelligence test?	Q 532 If I were to test a population of people taking care to sample a proportionate amount to the actual composition of the group, which kind of sampling would I be using?
Q 533 If I know something may be a confounding factor, and I create pairs of participants based on similar levels of this factor to eliminate its effect, this is called_____?	Q 534 counterbalancing
Q 535 Mary designed an experiment in which the groups were not randomly assigned and so the control and experimental groups were not the same, what kind of group design is this?	Q 536 If the results of my experiment are applicable to the entire population, my experiment is said to have _____ _.

A 529	A 530
The first intelligence test was created by Simon and Binet in 1905 for the purposes of ranking the intelligence of French children to select for mentally retarded children.	Intelligence quotient (IQ)
A 531	A 532
Lewis Terman	stratified random sampling
A 533	A 534
matched-subjects design	This is an experimental technique in which we make sure both the experimental and control group will experience both levels of the independent variable just at different times.
A 535	A 536
nonequivalent group design	external validity

Q 537

If I make inferences from a data set that go beyond the actual data points, this would be _____.

Q 538

A _____ is an extremely large or extremely small number that affects the measure of central tendency such that it is no longer accurately representative of the sample.

Q 539

T-score

Q 540

What is the difference between a positive correlation and a negative correlation?

Q 541

The _____ is the line one draws on the scatterplot to best represent the relationship between the two values.

Q 542

The _____ is the level of certainty we wish to have that there is an actual relationship between the two values in an experiment.

Q 543

The probability of making a type II error is measured by the _____ __.

Q 544

Which statistical test should I use if I am trying to compare three different groups or more?

A 537 inferential statistics	A 538 outlier
A 539 Similar to a Z-score T-score sets up a curve such that the mean is always 50 and each standard deviation is 10. You simply convert each number to the T-score value for easy comparison and analysis.	A 540 A positive correlation is one in which if one value increases the other value will increase. A negative correlation is one in which if one value decreases the other value increases.
A 541 line of best fit	A 542 alpha level / This is usually set at a 1 in 20 chance or an alpha level of 0.05.
A 543 beta level	A 544 analysis of variance (ANOVA)

Q 545 If I only have two groups to compare, which statistical test should I use?	Q 546 Chi-square tests are used for data that is _____ rather than numerical.
Q 547 What is the most common way to perform a meta-analysis?	Q 548 norm-referenced testing
Q 549 _____, rather than norm-referenced testing, determines how much information the test-taker knows about a certain subject, such as a history final.	Q 550 What are three things a test must have to be reliable?
Q 551 Split-half reliability, alternate-form, and test-retest method are three ways of establishing _____.	Q 552 validity

A 545	A 546
T-test	categorical

A 547	A 548
gather as many sources about the topic as possible examine for multiple themes publish the results of the meta-analysis for the larger community	A test in which one's score is compared to that of all of the other test-takers such as "Brian's score is in the 66th percentile."

A 549	A 550
Domain-referenced testing	dependability / consistency / repeatability

A 551	A 552
a test's reliability	how much a test measures what it claims to measure

Q 553

What would be the best way to test content validity?

Q 554

What does the face validity of the test show?

Q 555

What would be one way to determine the criterion validity of the SAT?

Q 556

construct validity

Q 557

Name two kinds of construct validity.

Q 558

What is the difference between aptitude and achievement tests?

Q 559

What would a personality inventory be likely to contain?

Q 560

The _____ is an intelligence test specially designed for children.

A 553	A 554
Examining the actual content of the test to make sure that it accurately and completely meets all of the facets of the construct that are being tested.	That the questions on the test will be asking questions that appear to ask questions about the subject of the test this is the least objective form of validity.

A 555	A 556
determine whether high scores on the SAT predict high GPAs in college	how well the test addresses what you were trying to measure

A 557	A 558
convergent validity / divergent validity	Someone's score on an aptitude test predicts future ability with training and growth someone's score on an achievement test shows how much s/he knows right now.

A 559	A 560
statements about personality / questions that assess likes and dislikes / self-selected ideals	Wechsler Intelligence Scale for Children (WISC)

Q 561

What are some special features of the Minnesota Multiphasic Personality Inventory?

Q 562

Which test is the California Personality Inventory the most like and why?

Q 563

Which projective test was specially designed for children?

Q 564

Rotter Incomplete Sentences Blank

Q 565

What is the theme of the Strong-Campbell Interest Inventory?

Q 566

What were Holland's six types of interests and occupational themes?

Q 567

What are four factors that can undermine data quality?

Q 568

What is the law of large numbers?

A 561 It has 10 clinical subscale scores including a score for carelessness faking and distorting.	A 562 The CPI is most like the MMPI but is especially intended for test takers ages 13 to young adult.
A 563 Blacky pictures	A 564 forty sentence stems that the test-taker fills out with whatever comes to mind
A 565 It is a career placement test based around the test-taker's interests.	A 566 realistic / investigative / artistic / social / enterprising / conventional
A 567 •Low precision of measurement / •The state of the participant / •The state of the experimenter / •Variation in the environment	A 568 (Unless there is significant sampling error) the larger the sample size the more reliable and valid the findings!

Q 569 **What are some arguments against using deception in psychological experiments?**	Q 570 **What is an attitude, and why is it so important to social psychology?**
Q 571 **According to social psychology, why do advertisers use the same commercial for the same product over and over again?**	Q 572 An ad with a political candidate explaining directly why he is better than his opponent is an example of what idea of social psychology?
Q 573 An ad featuring a beautiful model and a famous athlete using a product without saying why it is better than a competitor's product is an example of what idea in social psychology?	Q 574 **What compliance strategy believes a person should ask for something small to get something bigger later?**
Q 575 **If you ask your parents for $50 and they say no, then you ask them for $20 and they say yes, what compliance strategy is employed?**	Q 576 If I believe everyone likes chocolate because I like chocolate, and you believe everyone likes vanilla because you like vanilla, what is being exhibited?

A 569	A 570
–Informed consent for deception is not possible. / –When does the deception stop? / –Harms the credibility of psychology	An attitude is an evaluation of people objects or ideas. Since we can have positive or negative attitudes about nearly everything attitudes shape our view of the world.

A 571	A 572
The mere exposure effect hypothesizes that you will like something more as you see it more which will increase your likelihood of buying what is advertised.	This is an example of the central route of persuasion.

A 573	A 574
This is an example of the peripheral route to persuasion.	The foot-in-the-door phenomenon believes that if someone agrees to give away something small they will be more likely to give away something larger if it is requested later.

A 575	A 576
The door-in-the-face strategy suggests that if you ask for something large asking for something smaller will seem more reasonable and the request is more likely to be granted.	The false-consensus effect is occurring. We believe that because we feel one way about something everyone else feels the same way about it.

Q 577

What is a stereotype?

Q 578

What is prejudice and how does it differ from a stereotype?

Q 579

If you believe that other cultures are odd because they are not like your own, and that your culture is superior to other cultures, you are engaging in what?

Q 580

When prejudice is reduced through cooperation between groups to complete a larger goal, what is this goal called, and what is this belief?

Q 581

What is social facilitation?

Q 582

What is conformity?

Q 583

What are group norms?

Q 584

What may cause a person to riot when their favorite team wins a championship?

A 577	A 578
A stereotype is a shared belief or generalization about a group of people and can be positive or negative.	Prejudice is the negatively affective component of stereotyping like being scared of a group of people you believe (through stereotyping) to be violent.

A 579	A 580
ethnocentrism	This large shared goal is called a superordinate goal and the theory of minimizing prejudice through cooperation with other groups is called contact theory.

A 581	A 582
This is when the presence of one or more observers makes someone perform better at routine tasks.	It is the act of blending into a crowd or following along with an idea view or action of others.

A 583	A 584
Group norms are the rules of behavior (implicit or explicit) that go along with belonging to a group.	Deindividuation is the idea that people lose sight of their individual nature when they are excited (positively or negatively) and feel anonymous as they might feel being a part of a giant fanbase.

Q 585 Who performed the first official social psychology experiment?	**Q 586** Who was Kurt Lewin and what was his contribution to social psychology?
Q 587 What were two of Fritz Heider's major contributions to social psychology?	**Q 588** What is attribution theory?
Q 589 According to Fritz Heider, why do our feelings and beliefs tend to stay consistent over time?	**Q 590** What idea explains the difference in perspective between the person performing an action and the person observing the same action?
Q 591 Why are we more likely to take credit for our role in a successful group presentation than an unsuccessful group presentation?	**Q 592** Seeing a relationship between two unrelated things is called what?

A 585 Norman Triplett 1897 / He found that cyclists rode more slowly on their own than they did when other cyclists were riding with them.	A 586 He is frequently credited as being the "father of social psychology" and he derived field theory.
A 587 attribution theory / balance theory	A 588 Attribution theory is the attempt to understand events and behaviors by attributing intentions to others.
A 589 Balance theory states that people want to maintain psychological stasis so there is an urge to preserve attitudes through time.	A 590 actor-observer attributional divergence
A 591 The self-serving bias allows us to believe that we had a greater role in something's success than in its failure.	A 592 illusory correlation

Q 593	Q 594
The idea that one small belief change begets larger belief changes that ultimately snowball, making a large impact is known as what?	Studies have shown that doctors overestimate their ability to know the outcome of a case and that they claim after the fact to have "known it all along." What psychological effect is occurring?
Q 595	**Q 596**
What psychological effect is occurring when you believe a beautiful girl must also be smart and kind?	What did Lee Ross show in studies of people defending incorrect answers?
Q 597	**Q 598**
What is Richard Nisbett best known for?	What is base rate fallacy?
Q 599	**Q 600**
Who studied the illusion of control?	Using fuzzy trolls and rabbits' feet in bingo is an example of what?

A 593	A 594
slippery slope	hindsight bias
A 595	**A 596**
The halo effect is the belief that because a person has a good trait all their traits must also be good.	If a person was able to rationalize an incorrect answer before they learned it was false they would persist in their belief that the incorrect answer was actually true.
A 597	**A 598**
He is known for his studies showing that mental processes shape our preferences subconsciously and that we are unaware of why we do what we do.	Base rate fallacy is using irrelevant information and ignoring relevant information to make a decision or hypothesis.
A 599	**A 600**
Ellen Langer	Thinking you can control the outcome of something chance-based is known as the illusion of control.

Q 601

After a school shooting, people are quick to attribute one single, simple cause to the events, rather than believing a number of factors contributed. What is this an example of?

Q 602

What social psychologist is most closely associated with cognitive dissonance theory?

Q 603

What social psychologist is most closely linked with self-perception theory?

Q 604

How does Bem's self-perception theory contrast with Festinger's cognitive dissonance theory?

Q 605

Why would social psychology explain why we might like a rags-to-riches story more than a consistently happy story?

Q 606

Social exchange theory asserts that our interactions are such that they minimize _____ and maximize _____.

Q 607

What are the two facets of self-presentation?

Q 608

What is self-monitoring?

A 601 oversimplification / People will also persevere in their beliefs despite new information to the contrary.	A 602 Leon Festinger
A 603 Daryl Bem	A 604 Festinger believes that actions are born of beliefs rather than the other way around. Bem believes that people who are uncertain of their beliefs may consider their behavior for better understanding.
A 605 The gain-loss theory believes that we like "gain" more than consistency so a consistently happy story would have no "gain" and a rags-to-riches story would start sad but end up happy with more "gain."	A 606 costs rewards
A 607 self-monitoring / impression management / Self-presentation influences our behavior so that we are accepted by others.	A 608 when people pay attention to and modify their own behaviors often to be more favorable to others

Q 609

What is impression management?

Q 610

According to the theory of social facilitation, what helps or hinder performance on tasks?

Q 611

What did Robert Zajonc find about social facilitation?

Q 612

The process of evaluating your own abilities, actions, and ideas against others' are known as what?

Q 613

According to the theory of social comparison, why is mainstreaming children with disabilities a bad idea?

Q 614

According to Stanley Milgram, why would New Yorkers be considered rude and standoffish, as compared to people from less populated areas?

Q 615

Constant communication between people, or _____ _____ influences behavior.

Q 616

What theory states that a person who is grossly overpaid for his job will be more uncomfortable than a person who is fairly paid for his job?

A 609	A 610
acting in ways that are perceived favorably by others	the presence of others

A 611	A 612
Other people around improves performance on easy tasks but worsens performance on difficult tasks.	social comparison

A 613	A 614
Social comparisons are made to others in their immediate surroundings so children with disabilities might compare themselves to children without disabilities and develop low self-esteem.	The stimulus overload theory believes that people in densely populated areas are less prosocial because they have excessive stimuli and can't handle anymore.

A 615	A 616
reciprocal interaction	Equity theory asserts that we are most comfortable in situations where both rewards and punishments are equitable or logical.

Q 617

Who is known for his prisoner's dilemma and trucking company game studies?

Q 618

Within the context of conformity, what is the difference between compliance and acceptance?

Q 619

Within the context of conformity, what is a dissenter?

Q 620

What are the conditions under which conformity will not likely occur?

Q 621

Why do people take less individual responsibility for group actions as the group gets larger?

Q 622

According to Zimbardo, _____ behavior is increased in densely populated areas, based on his research with cars left in New York City and Palo Alto, CA.

Q 623

According to attraction and liking research, do opposites really attract?

Q 624

What allows feelings of emotional closeness to grow within a relationship?

A 617 Morton Deutsch	A 618 Compliance occurs when an individual conforms publicly but maintains a dissenting belief. Acceptance occurs when an individual conforms and does not have dissenting feelings.
A 619 A dissenter is a person who openly opposes the majority.	A 620 when it is obvious that the majority is trying to control reactance may occur / when people are forewarned that they are going to be controlled they withstand the pressure of conformity
A 621 As groups get larger there is a greater diffusion of responsibility among group members resulting from deindividuation. If nobody is an individual nobody takes individual responsibility.	A 622 antisocial
A 623 no	A 624 reciprocity of disclosure or sharing emotions feelings and secrets with one another

Q 625 **What are the two coping differentiations made by Richard Lazarus?**	Q 626 **What is objective self-awareness and what is its counterpart?**
Q 627 **What principle believes that people will get promoted at work until they reach a level where they become incompetent, and will ultimately remain in that position?**	Q 628 **What did Stuart Valins study, supporting the idea that the environment affects behavior?**
Q 629 **What did M. Rokeach find with regard to racial bias and belief similarity?**	Q 630 **What are the three parts of Fischbein and Ajzen's theory of reasoned action?**
Q 631 **Why is cross-cultural research important for psychology?**	Q 632 **According to Paul Ekman, what are the six basic emotions all humans have?**

A 625	A 626
problem-focused coping: changing the thing of creating stress / emotion-focused coping: changing the way you feel about the stressor by controlling emotions	It is the ability to attend to our thoughts actions feelings and selves and it is countered by deindividuation.

A 627	A 628
The Peter Principle	stress levels in differently shaped rooms

A 629	A 630
People want to be around others who have similar beliefs and attitudes rather than people with similar skin color.	behavioral intention=attitudes toward that behavior+subjective norms

A 631	A 632
Not all cultures are the same so before something can be considered normal or abnormal cultural variation must be taken into account to avoid improper generalization.	happiness / sadness / fear / disgust / anger / surprise

Q 633 What is the purpose of FACS coding?	Q 634 How did Walter Dill Scott help usher in the use of psychology in business?
Q 635 What term, used in industrial/organizational psychology, did Henry Landsberger coin in 1955?	Q 636 What term represents the interplay between humans and technology in work environments?
Q 637 A cost that will never be recovered and, therefore, should be ignored, is called what?	Q 638 Explain Bindle's role theory.
Q 639 What are the three types of cognitive dissonance?	Q 640 What kind of dissonance occurs when choosing between two or more positive options?

A 633 The Facial Action Coding System (FACS) is used to analyze facial expressions and sort them into emotion categories. It can also analyze whether a smile is genuinely reflective of emotion or not.	A 634 He used psychology in advertising to target consumers and he helped the military implement the use of psychological testing for personal purposes.
A 635 Hawthorne effect / The Hawthorne effect is the phenomenon where people increase workplace productivity if they believe they are being watched.	A 636 sociotechnical system
A 637 a sunk cost	A 638 This theory believes that people have an understanding of the roles they are supposed to fill and change their behavior to fit those roles.
A 639 free-choice dissonance / forced-compliance dissonance / post-decisional dissonance	A 640 free-choice dissonance

Q 641 When would forced-compliance dissonance occur?	Q 642 How does the spreading of alternatives reduce dissonance?
Q 643 What allows us to feel the emotions of others?	Q 644 What does Bandura's social learning theory suggest aggression?
Q 645 When someone stands in your "personal bubble," you tend to move away. What is the name for the study of personal space?	Q 646 phonemes
Q 647 morphemes	Q 648 phrase

A 641	A 642
when a person is forced to do something that conflicts with their existing attitudes or beliefs	It emphasizes the positive aspects of a chosen option. If trying to decide between two job applicants a manager will consider the one she chose to be smarter more capable etc. to reduce dissonance.
A 643	A 644
empathy	We learn aggression by observing it directly (modeling) or reinforcement which they believe will grant them a reward of some kind. / This research was done in the famous "Bobo doll" study.
A 645	A 646
proxemics	basic speech sounds with no meaning / ex. sh ph ee
A 647	A 648
the smallest carrier of meaning phonemes combined to create meaning	words grouped together to create a single unit of syntax in a sentence

Q 649 syntax	Q 650 grammar
Q 651 morphology	Q 652 prosody
Q 653 Who is considered the most important person in psycholinguistics?	Q 654 What did Chomsky's transformational grammar differentiate?
Q 655 You can change the _____ structure of a sentence without altering the _____ structure, or the meaning.	Q 656 Why would Chomsky say it is easier for children to learn a foreign language than adults?

A 649 an element of grammar that dictates the rules for phrase/sentence construction	A 650 rules for using a given language interrelating morphemes and syntax
A 651 grammar rules the understanding of how to group morphemes	A 652 the perception of tone inflections accents and emotional aspects of language that carry meaning
A 653 Noam Chomsky	A 654 surface structure and deep structure of language
A 655 surface deep	A 656 Because children have an inborn "language acquisition device" they are able to adapt to and incorporate new grammar rules into their own speech production.

Q 657 A child who calls every fuzzy, four-legged object a kitty is exhibiting what?	Q 658 "Me want cookie" is an example of what type of speech?
Q 659 This type of speech is comprised of one word that conveys the meaning of an entire sentence.	Q 660 Do boys or girls acquire language more quickly and accurately?
Q 661 Are children raised in bilingual environments faster or slower to learn the language?	Q 662 What parts of speech do children produce first?
Q 663 What did Roger Brown find regarding children's language acquisition?	Q 664 What did Katherine Nelson find regarding children's language acquisition?

A 657	A 658
overextension / Children frequently associate words with characteristics of an object without logically understanding the finer distinctions for example the ones between kitties and doggies.	telegraphic speech / A way to remember this is that the speaker lacks the flourish of a written letter but is instead barebones and only conveys necessity like a telegraph.

A 659	A 660
holophrastic speech / The one-word sentences are called holophrases.	girls

A 661	A 662
slower	nouns first then verbs / Telegraphic speech usually contains one of both like "mama go."

A 663	A 664
He found that children improve their understanding of language and grammar as they hypothesize about syntax and synthesize those hypotheses with their real-world language experience.	Children learn the language more rapidly after the onset of speech production (active speech) than they do while simply hearing it.

Q 665 Whose research on Ebonics found that it was not incorrect English, but rather a dialect with its own complex internal structure?	**Q 666** According to Vygotsky and Luria, do words mean the same thing to all people?
Q 667 How did Charles Osgood's semantic differential charts support Vygotsky and Luria's theory?	**Q 668** Where language acquisition was concerned, Chomsky is a _____.
Q 669 What is the learning theory of language?	**Q 670** William Sheldon's three personality types
Q 671 Ectomorph	**Q 672** An endomorph usually has a stout, round, often fatty, body type. These people tend to have what sorts of personality traits?

A 665	A 666
William Labov	No. They found that word meanings are different for different people affected by life experience.

A 667	A 668
They showed that people with related interests and backgrounds defined words similarly. / As Vygotsky and Luria posited different groups of people have different understandings of word connotations.	nativism / He argued that the capacity to acquire language was innate rather than learned.

A 669	A 670
Learning theory proposes that we learn language through conditioning and modeling. B.F. Skinner was a learning theorist.	endomorphy / ectomorphy / mesomorphy / These definitions of personality were based on body type.

A 671	A 672
In Sheldon's personality system ectomorphs are people with lanky-thin body-types. These people tend to be reserved introverted private and thoughtful.	a fun-loving nature / general good humor / affectionate / tolerance / relaxed

Q 673 Jeff is a man with large forearms and is generally fairly muscular. He is competitive, adventurous, courageous, and often takes risks, which of Sheldon's personality types does he fit?	Q 674 humanism
Q 675 psychodynamic theory	Q 676 Name three components in Freud's structural psychoanalytic theory of personality.
Q 677 What are the four broad theories of personality?	Q 678 What are the defining characteristics of stage theories?
Q 679 What are the stages of Freud's psychosexual stage theory?	Q 680 Freud referred to life energy as _____.

A 673	A 674
Mesomorph	Humanism is a theory of personality psychology that emphasizes humans' free will and focuses on therapy that is client-centered.

A 675	A 676
This theory was created by Sigmund Freud. It hypothesized that forces in the unconscious mind define one's personality and control behaviors and emotions.	id / ego / superego

A 677	A 678
psychoanalytic / humanistic / social-cognitive / trait theories	Stage theories believe people develop in stages or steps in the same order without skipping a step and one stage can be distinguished from all other stages.

A 679	A 680
oral stage (birth to one year) / anal stage (one to three years) / phallic stage (three to five years) / latency stage (six years to puberty) / genital stage (puberty onward)	libido

Q 681 **This level, just below the level of conscious awareness, contains thoughts, memories, feelings, and images that are easily recalled.**	**Q 682** Freud believed in dream analysis, he composed a list of _____, items or events that appeared in dreams but in reality represent other items or events in the subconscious.
Q 683 **On which principle does the id operate?**	**Q 684** **The superego, the acknowledged opposite of the _____, is an internal representation of society's rules, morals, and obligations.**
Q 685 **The_____ and the _____ are two subsystems of the superego.**	**Q 686** **Name two things that the ego allows us to accomplish in everyday life?**
Q 687 **On which principle does the ego operate?**	**Q 688** **What is the reality principle?**

A 681	A 682
preconscious	Freudian symbols

A 683	A 684
the pleasure principle / The id seeks to maximize pleasure while minimizing pain.	id

A 685	A 686
conscience ego-ideal	functioning in the environment / acting logically

A 687	A 688
the reality principle	the set of desires that can be satisfied only if the means to satisfy them exists and is available

Q 689

What kind of thought is the ego most involved in?

Q 690

What is the purpose of defense mechanisms?

Q 691

When I say, "Maggie is afraid of spiders" when, in reality, I am afraid of spiders, I am employing which defense mechanism?

Q 692

Repression, a type of defense mechanism, describes the process by which anxiety-provoking memories or desires are moved to the _____.

Q 693

If, after an argument, a child shows anger not towards his friend, with whom he is angry, but to a stuffed animal, what defense mechanism is he exhibiting?

Q 694

suppression

Q 695

In _____, the ego completely reverses a desire to make itself safer or more socially acceptable.

Q 696

What defense mechanism uses logic to excuse emotional or irrational behavior?

| A 689

conscious thought | A 690

The purpose of defense mechanisms is to manage anxiety produced by the id-superego conflict. |
|---|---|
| A 691

projection | A 692

subconscious |
| A 693

displacement | A 694

Suppression is the Freudian defense mechanism that involves deliberate forgetting of anxiety-provoking material. |
| A 695

reaction formation | A 696

rationalization |

Q 697 **Regression involves reverting to what kind of behaviors?**	**Q 698** Which defense mechanism involves the channeling or redirecting of sexual or aggressive feelings into a more socially acceptable outlet?
Q 699 **What describes man's inherent envy towards a woman's ability to nurture and sustain life?**	**Q 700** _____, a system initially outlined by Sigmund Freud, is a kind of long-term psychotherapy that involves uncovering unconscious/repressed conflicts that arose in psychosexual development
Q 701 **Typically, what does psychoanalytic assessment involve?**	**Q 702** If I say "knife" and encourage my patient to say any words s/he may associate with that word, no matter how unrelated they may seem, I am trying to use what psychoanalytic technique?
Q 703 **Freud developed a system of dream interpretation based on what premise?**	**Q 704** **What are some indications that a patient is exhibiting resistance to psychoanalysis?**

A 697	A 698
childish behaviors	sublimation

A 699	A 700
womb envy	Psychoanalysis

A 701	A 702
a one-on-one therapist and patient relationship in which the therapist uses techniques (such as free association and dream recall) to gain access to the unconscious	free association

A 703	A 704
The dreaming mind is more relaxed so that the unconscious desires and repressions can be revealed through dream analysis.	missing sessions / unwillingness to free associate / withholding dream information / refusal to participate in therapeutic activities / changing topics

Q 705

transference

Q 706

The emotions that the therapist develops toward a patient are called _____.

Q 707

In Karen Horney's theory of personality, what is important in forming the basis of the adult personality?

Q 708

What characterizes basic anxiety, the main tenet in Karen Horney's theory of personality?

Q 709

How does one overcome basic anxiety in Karen Horney's psychological system?

Q 710

Carl Jung's theory of personality is based on the idea that the mind comprises pairs of _____.

Q 711

What, according to Carl Jung's theory, is the persona?

Q 712

Carl Jung would describe the dark, passionate, more primordial parts of someone as that person's _____.

A 705 The feelings and behaviors that the patient develops for the therapist that are reflections of past and current relationships.	A 706 countertransference
A 707 interactions between the child and the parent as the child deals with basic anxiety	A 708 the feeling of being alone in an unfamiliar or hostile world
A 709 withdrawal from people who provoke basic anxiety / the deliberate movement towards people who remove basic anxiety / conflict with people who can be overcome	A 710 opposing forces
A 711 the mask that each person presents to the outside world	A 712 shadow

Q 713

According to Jung, each person contains a female and a male side to our personality, or an _____ and _____.

Q 714

According to Jung's theory, what is the purpose of the self?

Q 715

What are the two divisions of unconsciousness in Jung's theory?

Q 716

What comprises the personal unconsciousness?

Q 717

What can be found in the collective unconscious?

Q 718

Archetypes, found in the collective unconscious, are characterized as what?

Q 719

Which personality psychologist's system of extroversion and introversion inspired the Myers-Briggs personality test?

Q 720

Alfred Adler's theory of personality speculated that children develop feelings of _____ due to their size and level of competence, and they spend the rest of their lives trying to overcome it.

A 713	A 714
anima animus	to balance the opposing forces and the desires of the mind
A 715	**A 716**
personal unconsciousness / collective unconscious	repressed memories and clusters of thought
A 717	**A 718**
behavior and memory common to all humans and passed down from our ancient and common ancestors archetypes	the behaviors and memories in the collective unconscious / These are usually emotionally-laden thoughts or images.
A 719	**A 720**
Carl Jung / This system also included: thinking feeling sensing and intuiting.	inferiority

Q 721 According to Adler, the best way to overcome inferiority is through development of _____, failure to do so could result in the development of a(n) _____.	Q 722 fictional finalism
Q 723 creative self	Q 724 Alfred Adler described a system called _____ in which someone's unique way of achieving superiority was reflected in the personal choices s/he made.
Q 725 _____ personality treatments are based on present life situations and interpersonal relationships.	Q 726 Ego psychology is:
Q 727 Who identified the defense mechanisms?	Q 728 What is the object-relations theory?

A 721 social interest inferiority complex	A 722 According to Alfred Adler people are more motivated by their fictional expectations for the future than they are by past experiences.
A 723 the unique qualities within someone that help them express a personality in a singular way	A 724 style of life
A 725 Neo-Freudian	A 726 a form of psychoanalytic theory in which the most important element was the ego as it related to the conscious world.
A 727 Anna Freud	A 728 a psychodynamic system in which children create and develop internalized symbols or objects which are significant representations of their personalities

Q 729 **Name 4 object-relations psychologists**	Q 730 **What do the humanistic theories of personality emphasize?**
Q 731 **What two aspects do the humanistic theories focus on?**	Q 732 **According to Abraham Maslow's humanist perspective, what is the ultimate purpose for existence?**
Q 733 **What characterizes self-actualization?**	Q 734 **Name two humanistic theorists.**
Q 735 **Maslow's hierarchy of needs**	Q 736 **What is the self-concept?**

A 729	A 730
Otto Kernberg / Margaret Mahler / Melanie Klein / D.W. Winnicott	the uniqueness and richness of being human
A 731	**A 732**
subjective reality / subjective mental events	self-actualization
A 733	**A 734**
creatively becoming the person you are capable of being to your highest potential / Very few people reach this level in Maslow's system.	Abraham Maslow / Carl Rogers
A 735	**A 736**
physiological / safety / love/belonging / esteem / self-actualization	the mental representation of who we feel we truly are

Q 737

According to Rogers, _____ distort our self-concept

Q 738

In Rogerian theory, _____ is a trait of the therapist that creates a system in which the client feels safe and can speak freely.

Q 739

If I encourage my patient to look for life's meanings through making personal choices, I am using what kind of therapy?

Q 740

What do social-cognitive theories assume about personality?

Q 741

In social-cognitive theory, how are constructs developed and modified?

Q 742

Albert Bandura focused on the idea of _____ as central to personality.

Q 743

What does self-efficacy encompass?

Q 744

Which social-cognitive theory of personality, proposed by Julian Rotter, believes that effort has a major role in personality?

A 737 conditions of worth	A 738 unconditional positive regard
A 739 humanist-existential therapy	A 740 that cognitive constructs are the basis of the personality
A 741 through learning in social environments	A 742 self-efficacy
A 743 one's beliefs about his/her own abilities in a given situation	A 744 locus of control theory

Q 745

According to trait theorists, traits are largely _____ rather than acquired through experience.

Q 746

What are the big five personality traits?

Q 747

What are the two methods of trait research analysis?

Q 748

What is the main difference between nomothetic and idiographic traits?

Q 749

According to Gordon Allport, what are the three types of traits?

Q 750

According to Allport, a trait that overrides one's whole being is a _____, while _____ are the person's primary characteristics, and traits that constitute interests are _____.

Q 751

If I used to shop because I needed clothes and now I shop because I simply enjoy shopping, this activity is said to have attained_____.

Q 752

The theory that we try to make sense of the world by generating, testing, and revising hypotheses about our social reality, was developed by George Kelly. It is known as what?

A 745	A 746
inherited	openness/non-openness / conscientiousness/undirectedness / extroversion/introversion / agreeableness/antagonism / neuroticism/stability / (Use the acronym OCEAN to remember the big five!)
A 747	**A 748**
nomothetic analysis / idiographic analysis	Nomothetic traits are thought to be universal (i.e. the big five) while idiographic traits are unique to the individual.
A 749	**A 750**
cardinal / central / secondary	cardinal trait central traits secondary
A 751	**A 752**
functional autonomy	personal construct theory

Q 753

Which theorist is known for recognizing that traits often vary depending on circumstances?

Q 754

Hans Eysenck used factor analysis to identify common behavioral traits along three dimensions. What are they?

Q 755

_____ was a personality psychologist who used factor analysis to determine 16 basic traits that make the building blocks of personality.

Q 756

Raymond Cattel believed that _____, the person's underlying characteristics, were the basis of personality and gave rise to _____.

Q 757

Used primarily by psychoanalysts, _____ present ambiguous stimuli (i.e. inkblots) with the assumption that test takers will project their unconscious thoughts onto the stimuli.

Q 758

What research effect observes that individuals will claim general descriptions of their personality (that can apply to a wide range of people) are highly accurate?

Q 759

behaviorist theory of personality

Q 760

_____ and _____ were behaviorist psychologists who examined stimulus-responses and conflicting motivations as the basis for personality development.

A 753	A 754
Walter Mischel	extroversion-introversion / neuroticism-stability / psychoticism
A 755	A 756
Raymond Cattell	source traits surface traits
A 757	A 758
projective personality tests	Barnum effect / (The effect is named after P.T. Barnum)
A 759	A 760
This theory places an emphasis on behavior as the source of personality: people develop based on their interactions with their environments.	John Dollard Neal Miller

Q 761 **Albert Bandura's system used what theory of personality development?**	Q 762 **Kurt Lewin's field theory of personality psychology emphasized_____**
Q 763 **Herman Witkin tied _____ to personality by differentiating between people who make specified responses based on stimuli and those who have difficulty differentiating answers based on specific stimuli.**	Q 764 **People who are high in the personality trait "Machiavellianism" tend to:**
Q 765 **Sandra Bem's theory is based on a personality test in which _____ and _____ are measured and assessed.**	Q 766 **androgyny**
Q 767 **rational-emotive theory**	Q 768 **The life-span perspective of developmental psychology defines it as what?**

A 761 social learning theory / This theory states that people's personalities develop as a reflection of the behavioral models they encounter during their lives.	A 762 a personality that was dynamic and in flux he did not believe in static traits.
A 763 field-dependence	A 764 be excellent manipulators and tend to believe they know what's best for others
A 765 masculinity femininity	A 766 Within Sandra Bem's system it is the characteristic of having a personality that is both feminine and masculine.
A 767 This is a combination of emotion cognitive and behavioral aspects of psychology that operates from the belief that thoughts together with feelings create behaviors.	A 768 the study of changes in abilities thoughts and behaviors that occur as one age

Q 769	Q 770
Which pervasive debate in developmental psychology deals with the extent to which heredity and the environment each influence behavior?	nature

Q 771	Q 772
_____ is the half of the nature vs. nurture debate that states one's development is based entirely in the experiences and environment that person has.	What is the difference between life-span psychologists and child psychologists?

Q 773	Q 774
What is defined as the typical sequence of developmental changes for a group of people?	Describe the cross-sectional method.

Q 775	Q 776
Describe the longitudinal method.	Describe the cohort effect.

A 769	A 770
nature vs. nurture debate	As part of the nature vs. nurture debate people who emphasize nature believe that people develop based on unique qualities inherent in their genetic code.
A 771	A 772
Nurture	both study development but child psychologists focus on the earlier portion of the life-span
A 773	A 774
normative development	this method compares groups of people of different ages on similar tasks
A 775	A 776
involves following a small group of people over a long portion of their lives assessing change at set intervals	when there are differences in the experiences of each age group as a result of growing up in different historical times

Q 777

In which study method are cross-sectional groups assessed at least two times over a span of months or years?

Q 778

What is maturation?

Q 779

From the maturation perspective of development, what is the benefit of the greater preprogrammed physiological development of the brain?

Q 780

Continuous development is gradual.

Q 781

One example of stage-oriented, or _____, learning is experiencing a growth spurt.

Q 782

The time during which a skill or ability must develop is referred to as the _____.

Q 783

What are the two divisions of culture in developmental psychology?

Q 784

Which type of culture promotes personal needs above the needs of society?

A 777	A 778
cohort-sequential studies	biological readiness
A 779 more complex conceptualization and reasoning	**A 780** true / One example of continuous development is social skill building.
A 781 discontinuous	**A 782** critical period
A 783 collectivism / individualist	**A 784** individualist / Western cultures are typically viewed as individualist cultures.

Q 785

What do collectivist cultures emphasize?

Q 786

Stages are patterns of behavior that occur in a _____.

Q 787

How do the developmental stages of psychology work?

Q 788

What are the three realms of development?

Q 789

What six reflexes is the neonate equipped with?

Q 790

When I put my finger in a neonate's hand and she grabs it, this exemplifies which reflex?

Q 791

According to the Babinski reflex, what response will an infant have to be stroked on the bottom of the foot?

Q 792

When an infant's head is suddenly moved, the infant's limbs will splay out, they will extend their limbs, and then hug themselves. This exemplifies which infantile reflex?

A 785	A 786
the needs of society which are placed before the needs of the individual / Many Asian cultures are considered collectivist cultures.	fixed sequence
A 787	**A 788**
each stage has a unique set of cognitive structures (or sets of mental abilities) that build on the cognitive structures established in the previous stage such that one cannot skip a step	physical / cognitive / social
A 789	**A 790**
sucking reflex / palmar reflex / Babinski reflex / head-turning (rooting) reflex / Moro reflex / orienting reflex	palmar reflex
A 791	**A 792**
the toes will splay out	the Moro reflex

Q 793

What is the head-turning, or rooting, reflex?

Q 794

Which reflex is triggered by placing something in the baby's mouth?

Q 795

_____ refers to the development of learning, memory, reasoning, and problem-solving.

Q 796

Jean Piaget's developmental theory is based on what concept?

Q 797

What is one way through which children attempt to reach equilibration, according to Piaget's theory?

Q 798

Assimilation involves incorporating new ideas into already-existing mental representations, or _____.

Q 799

What process must a child undergo when faced with information that does not easily fit into an existing schema?

Q 800

What are Piaget's stages of development?

A 793	A 794
the response elicited by touching the baby's cheek	the sucking reflex

A 795	A 796
Cognitive development	a child's attempt to reach a balance between what he encounters in the environment and what cognitive structures he brings to the situation (equilibration)

A 797	A 798
assimilation- understanding new information based on a pre-existing schema	schemas

A 799	A 800
accommodation	sensorimotor / pre-operational / concrete operational / formal operational

Q 801

Reflexive reactions and circular reactions (repeated behaviors through which the infant manipulates the environment) are typical in which of Piaget's stages of development?

Q 802

The pre-operational stage of Piaget's theory of development is characterized by the shift to _____, the ability to use words to substitute for objects.

Q 803

What two important concepts appear during Piaget's concrete operational stage?

Q 804

Reversibility

Q 805

Which stage in Piaget's stages of development is characterized by the presence of theoretical thinking?

Q 806

If a toy disappears from a child's field of view, the child will continue to look for it. This exemplifies the development of which process during the sensorimotor stage?

Q 807

The inability to see the world from anyone else's point of view is _____.

Q 808

If your nephew believes that his stuffed animal is alive, he is subscribing to what belief, found in Piaget's pre-operational stage?

A 801	A 802
sensorimotor stage	symbolic thinking

A 803	A 804
reversibility / conservation	This is the understanding that many mathematical and practical operations can be reversed.

A 805	A 806
formal operational stage	object permanence

A 807	A 808
egocentrism	animism

Q 809

What two abilities does a child at Piaget's formal operational stage acquire?

Q 810

What is metacognition?

Q 811

How do psychologists test theory of mind?

Q 812

Who was the theorist responsible for stressing social factors as critical for developmental processes?

Q 813

What is internalization?

Q 814

According to Vygotsky, the _____ is the range between the developed level of ability that a child displays and the potential level of ability of which the child is capable.

Q 815

Vygotsky proposed that a child realizes his potential through a process that allows him to move across the zone of proximal development by being helped by a peer. Name this process.

Q 816

Which theorist is credited with successfully championing the view that development occurs across an entire lifetime?

A 809	A 810
metacognition / hypothetical reasoning	the ability to recognize one's cognitive processes and change or adapt those processes if necessary
A 811	A 812
false-belief task	Lev Vygotsky
A 813	A 814
Internalization is the absorption of knowledge into the self from environmental and social contexts.	zone of proximal development
A 815	A 816
scaffolding	Erik Erikson

Q 817

Which theorist developed a theory that viewed development as a series of "conflicts" that must be resolved?

Q 818

Name and describe the first stage in Erikson's psychosocial stage theory.

Q 819

Which of Erikson's stages is marked by potty training and temper tantrums?

Q 820

If your little brother asks, "why?" about everything you do, which of Erikson's stages is he likely in?

Q 821

What psychosocial stage begins in first grade, and is characterized by children comparing themselves to others more regularly than before (meaning they need more positive reinforcement)?

Q 822

The successful resolution of which one of Erikson's stages results in infidelity or truthfulness to oneself?

Q 823

From around 21-40 years of age, we attempt to find and navigate meaningful relationships. What stage is this?

Q 824

Which stage occurs during old age and involves coming to terms with successes and failures?

A 817	A 818
Erik Erikson	trust vs. mistrust / During this time babies learn whether they can trust their environment and their caregivers to provide them with the things they need for survival.
A 819	**A 820**
autonomy vs. shame and doubt / This is the stage when children begin asserting their control over their bodies and behaviors usually ages 1-3 years old.	initiative vs. Guilt / This is the stage where children try to understand the world around them and asking questions helps them solve problems ages 3-6.
A 821	**A 822**
industry vs. inferiority	identity vs. role confusion
A 823	**A 824**
intimacy vs. isolation	integrity vs. despair

Q 825

Which 1950s researcher was able to demonstrate that rhesus monkeys need comfort and security just as much as food?

Q 826

John Bowlby is considered to be the father of what theory?

Q 827

What tendency is defined as the preference of specific familiar individuals over others in infants?

Q 828

Describe the idea of self-referencing.

Q 829

According to Mary Ainsworth, there are three types of infant attachment patterns. What are they?

Q 830

This type of attachment, in which the child uses the parent for support, is the most common. What is it?

Q 831

What behaviors are consistent with anxiously/ambivalently attached babies in a strange situation experiment?

Q 832

Mary Ainsworth studied infant attachment using the "strange situation." What is a "strange situation"?

A 825	A 826
Harry Harlow	attachment theory

A 827	A 828
attachment	Self-referencing is to observe the behavior of others in social situations to obtain information or guidance.

A 829	A 830
secure / insecure/resistant / insecure/avoidant / There is also a "disorganized" type of attachment in which the child behaves erratically.	secure attachment

A 831	A 832
These babies often show signs of distress when parents leave the room but resist or refuse to comfort from them when they return.	the parent or primary guardian leaves a child with a stranger and then returns observing behavior in absentia. This allows researchers to see the infant's style of attachment.

Q 833

Name the three types of parenting styles.

Q 834

If a child is routinely spanked for disobedience and lacks curiosity and decision-making capabilities, what parenting style do her parents most likely identify with?

Q 835

What style of parenting is consistent with a lack of defined rules or rules that are inconsistently enforced?

Q 836

Elisabeth Kubler-Ross pioneered a theory of social development about the stages of death and dying in which she identified stages of grief. What are the stages?

Q 837

List the six stages and motivators of Kohlberg's moral schema.

Q 838

Level one of Kohlberg's theory of moral development occurs between ages 7 and 10 and is identified by what two-stage system of moral judgment?

Q 839

What does the Heinz dilemma test?

Q 840

What is the difference between stage one and stage two of Kohlberg's stages of preconventional morality?

A 833	A 834
authoritarian / authoritative / permissive	authoritarian

A 835	A 836
permissive parenting	denial / anger / bargaining / depression / acceptance

A 837	A 838
Stage1: obedience and punishment / Stage 2: Self-interest / Stage 3: conformity and seeking social approval / Stage 4: social order / Stage 5: social contract / Stage 6: universal principles	preconventional morality

A 839	A 840
The way in which the participant defends his/her answers determines which phase of morality they are in.	In stage one children make judgments motivated by fear whereas in stage two they make judgments by evaluating benefits and reciprocity.

Q 841

Kohlberg's level two of moral development is characterized by the utilization of _____ _ or the internalization of society's rules and morals.

Q 842

In Kohlberg's third level of moral development, which occurs from around age 16 on, the individual adheres to post-conventional morality, which is characterized by what?

Q 843

Carol Gilligan revised Kohlberg's theory in order to place emphasis on the development of _____ as central to moral progress as more important to the moral reasoning of women.

Q 844

What did Martin and Halverson propose regarding gender schematic processing theory?

Q 845

Bandura believed that sexual roles are acquired through social or vicarious learning so that each successive generation provides the model for the following generation.

Q 846

Puberty is a sexual maturation, marked by the onset of what ability?

Q 847

Emerging during puberty, _____ _, such as the growth of reproductive organs, develop.

Q 848

In women, widening of the hips and breast development would be two features of _____ .

A 841	A 842
conventional morality	the development of an internal set of values that may generate occasional conflict with societal values
A 843	A 844
caring relationships	They proposed that once children label themselves with a gender they begin to pay more attention to that gender's behaviors and stop paying as much attention to the behaviors of the opposite gender.
A 845	A 846
TRUE	the ability to reproduce
A 847	A 848
primary sex characteristics	secondary sex characteristics

Q 849	Q 850
Thomas Hobbes, James Mill, David Hume, and George Berkeley were all members of the British empiricist school of thought, what did these philosophers believe about development?	Which French philosopher espoused his belief that society is unnecessary to a child's development?

Q 851	Q 852
What did Charles Darwin contribute to the changing of the developmental psychological thought?	What work earned G. Stanley Hall the title of "Father of Developmental Psychology"?

Q 853	Q 854
The psychologist _____ emphasized the role of the environment in shaping a child's behavior, especially the importance of parents in creating well-formed children.	Describe Arnold Gesell's theory of development.

Q 855	Q 856
Who invented the science of genetics?	genes

A 849 That one gains knowledge through experience the more experiences you give a child the more knowledge s/he will have as an adult.	A 850 Jean-Jacques Rousseau
A 851 He contributed detailed observational books of the developmental progress of children which detailed the relationship between the environment and the individual's changes to adapt to the	A 852 He developed and tested a series of questionnaires for children of different ages and he was the founder of the American Psychological Association.
A 853 John B. Watson	A 854 Gesell believed that a child's development was a biological process that has predictable stages that occur at differ paces for each child.
A 855 Gregor Mendel	A 856 the basic piece of heredity

Q 857

Alternate forms of genes are called?

Q 858

For each allele, there is both a _____ and _____ copy of each allele.

Q 859

The _____ of a person is the exact series of genes in their biological code. The _____ is a person's visible traits.

Q 860

Each human being has all of their genes located on _____ pairs of _____.

Q 861

Monozygotic twins share fifty percent of the same genetic material.

Q 862

_____ twins share fifty percent of the same genetic material, just like non-twin siblings.

Q 863

Which psychologist created a huge longitudinal study comparing the IQs and behaviors of highly intelligent children with normative children in the general population?

Q 864

What are the characteristics of Down's syndrome?

A 857	A 858
alleles	dominant recessive

A 859	A 860
genotype phenotype	23 chromosomes

A 861	A 862
FALSE	Dizygotic

A 863	A 864
Lewis Terman	a genetic anomaly an extra 21st chromosome and mental retardation

Q 865

Two gametes, or human sex cells, fuse to form a

_____.

Q 866

What are the three phases of gestation that the zygote experiences?

Q 867

During the _____ phase, the zygote begins to divide and is eventually implanted in the uterine wall. This whole phase takes about two weeks.

Q 868

Describe the embryonic phase of prenatal development.

Q 869

During which stage of gestation does the zygote experience rapid growth, movement, and sexual differentiation?

Q 870

babbling

Q 871

What did Lenneberg, Rebelsky, and Nichols discover about babbling that influenced developmental psychology?

Q 872

Noam Chomsky believed that children had an internal ability to acquire language, which was gathered through a region of the brain called the _____ _.

A 865	A 866
zygote	germinal stage / embryonic stage / fetal stage

A 867	A 868
germinal	During this phase the embryo increases in size rapidly it begins to develop fingers toes and genitals.

A 869	A 870
the fetal phase	the sounds an infant makes that form the precursor to language

A 871	A 872
They discovered that all children babble whether they are deaf or can hear. Deaf children stop verbally babbling but will "babble" with their hands in a precursor to sign language.	language acquisition device (LAD)

Q 873 **At what age do children begin adding multiple words together? At what age do they begin using simple sentences?**	**Q 874** **categorical perception**
Q 875 When toddlers say things like "the cat ruined" when they previously said "the cat ran" after learning about past tense verbs, this is an example of _____.	**Q 876** **According to Alexander Thomas and Stella Chess, what are the three kinds of infant temperaments?**
Q 877 **Name three research methods that are most commonly used for studying infants.**	**Q 878** **social smiling**
Q 879 **Imprinting**	**Q 880** **Who was Philippe Pinel?**

A 873	A 874
18-20 months 2.5-3 years old	the ability that infants have to denote different kinds of sounds that either differentiate meaning or do not

A 875	A 876
errors of growth	easy slow to warm up and difficult

A 877	A 878
observing infant behavior in the laboratory / observing infants in natural settings such as the home / from reports written by the parents/ caregivers	It is the ability of young infants to smile as a method of communication before they can talk. After five months of age only familiar faces will cause the baby to exhibit a social smile.

A 879	A 880
Imprinting is the process by which baby birds and other creatures recognize and become attached to their caregivers such as when baby birds learn to recognize and bond with their mothers from birth.	Pinel was one of the first mental health professionals to treat his patients with compassion and kindness. The model set by the Parisian hospital he ran was adopted by many other asylums.

Q 881 **Which American activist fought for asylum reform in the mid-1800s?**	Q 882 **Who wrote The Myth of Mental Illness?**
Q 883 **dysphoria**	Q 884 **anhedonia**
Q 885 **What are the components of Beck's Negative Cognitive Triad?**	Q 886 **bipolar disorder**
Q 887 **What are the major characteristics of cyclothymic disorder?**	Q 888 In bulimia nervosa, someone will have multiple large eating binges and then compensate for the binges with: _____, _____, or _____.

A 881	A 882
Dorothea Dix	Thomas Szasz

A 883	A 884
An unusually high level of negative mood	An unusually low level of positive mood inability to feel pleasure.

A 885	A 886
Negative views of the self: e.g. "I suck." / Negative views of the world: e.g. "Everybody hates me." / Negative views of the future: e.g." My life will always suck."	This mental disorder is characterized by periods of depression and mania.

A 887	A 888
one or more periods of hypomanic symptoms interspersed with one or more periods of depressive symptoms.	purging excessive exercise fasting / However if the individual also meets criteria for anorexia nervosa you diagnose anorexia nervosa (binging and purging subtype) instead.

Q 889 Is there a gender difference in the incidence of anorexia nervosa?	**Q 890** Is Asperger's Syndrome a valid DSM-5 diagnosis?
Q 891 Do all people who have autism also have an intellectual disability?	**Q 892** personality disorder
Q 893 Which personality disorder is characterized by a blatant disregard for the rights or interests of others which is usually manifested through repeated illegal acts and aggression towards others?	**Q 894** What are the key features of narcissistic personality disorder?
Q 895 borderline personality disorder	**Q 896** If a patient exhibited excessive emotional reactions to normal, every-day stimuli, and was preoccupied with the constant need for attention, what personality disorder would you most likely diagnose?

A 889	A 890
Yes! Anorexia nervosa is much more common among females. It is estimated that for every 1 male with AN there are 10 females.	No. / In the DSM-IV the diagnosis Asperger's Syndrome (a very high functioning form of autism) has been subsumed into the diagnosis of Autism Spectrum Disorder.
A 891	**A 892**
No. Although it is common for people who have autism to have an intellectual disability many individuals who meet criteria for autism do not meet criteria for intellectual disability.	A disorder characterized by the pervasive expression of extreme abnormal personality constructs that interfere with normal social functioning.
A 893	**A 894**
antisocial personality disorder	Exaggerated self-importance / The excessive constant need for others' admiration / Lack of empathy for others
A 895	**A 896**
This personality disorder is one of the more volatile personality disorders it is characterized by interpersonal issues identify problems fear of abandonment and often self-injurious behavior.	histrionic personality disorder

Q 897 _____ personality disorder is characterized by extreme distrust and suspicion of others.	Q 898 Which personality disorder is associated with little emotional expression and a lack of social interactions?
Q 899 What is the defining characteristic of dependent personality disorder?	Q 900 Describe the active phase of schizophrenia.
Q 901 What is a delusion?	Q 902 If a patient believes he is supernaturally powerful, wealthy, or famous, what may he be suffering from?
Q 903 What is a delusion of persecution?	Q 904 dementia praecox

A 897	A 898
Paranoid	schizoid personality disorder

A 899	A 900
the need to be cared for	This is the period of time (usually 6 months or more) in which the patient exhibits a mixture of positive and negative schizophrenic symptoms.

A 901	A 902
A fixed belief that is not amenable to change in light of conflicting evidence	delusions of grandeur

A 903	A 904
The unfounded belief that you are being or will be harmed these delusions usually involve the mentally ill person believing they are the center of a plot.	This was the original name for schizophrenia which literally means early dementia.

Q 905

List some examples of positive symptoms associated with schizophrenia.

Q 906

What is the lifetime prevalence of schizophrenia?

Q 907

The diagnosis _____ is used to describe individuals who have features of both schizophrenia and severe mood disorder

Q 908

Name the two phases of schizophrenia

Q 909

Not all _____ is a sign of mental illness. For example, if you have a migraine, you may see spots in your field of vision.

Q 910

What is the most common type of hallucination?

Q 911

The periods of time in an individual with schizophrenia in which s/he is not actively psychotic but has already had a schizophrenic episode are usually called _____.

Q 912

In_____ schizophrenia, the symptom onset is usually sudden and deep, but the prognosis is usually good.

A 905 delusions / hallucinations / disorganized behavior / disorganized speech / catatonic behavior	A 906 Slightly over 1 %.
A 907 Schizoaffective disorder	A 908 prodromal phase / active phase
A 909 hallucinations	A 910 Auditory hallucinations are the most common types of hallucinations such as hearing voices but hallucinations can occur in any of the five sensory modalities.
A 911 residual schizophrenia	A 912 reactive

Q 913

Sam presents at your office claiming symptoms that have lasted for about six months. He presents with hallucinations, delusions, disorganized speech, and flat affect. What mental disease does he have?

Q 914

What are three common features of schizophrenic disorders?

Q 915

If Jim's schizophrenia has a slow and insidious onset, what is this called and what is his prognosis?

Q 916

Who coined the term schizophrenia?

Q 917

What is waxy flexibility?

Q 918

_____ affect is characterized by very few expressions of affect and _____ affect is characterized by consistently manifesting socially unacceptable emotional expressions.

Q 919

If a patient presented with involuntary, uncontrollable, intrusive thoughts that she unsuccessfully tried to control through repetitive behaviors or rituals, which disorder would she have?

Q 920

What is the cardinal symptom of trichotillomania?

A 913	A 914
schizophrenia	delusions / hallucinations / disturbed or innapropriate emotional responses to environmental stimuli
A 915	**A 916**
process schizophrenia his prognosis is poor as it shows a long-term deterioration	Eugene Bleuler / Bleuler identified the lack of coherence between emotion and thought and the breaking away from reality characteristic of psychotic illness.
A 917	**A 918**
Waxy flexibility is a catatonia symptom in which the body can be moved into new positions and will stay there instead of going limp.	Flat inappropriate
A 919	**A 920**
obsessive-compulsive disorder	Pulling out one's hair. / In the DSM-5 trichotillomania is recognized as an OCD-spectrum disorder. (Previously it was considered an impulse control disorder.)

Q 921 **Name two cognitive mechanisms that contribute to the anxious apprehension experienced by people who have an anxiety disorder:**	Q 922 **Feelings of dread and worry, along with constant autonomic nervous system arousal, characterize which disorder?**
Q 923 **People who have been exposed to high levels of violence, such as soldiers in war, are at risk for developing which disorder, characterized by recurring thoughts and anxiety linked to that trauma?**	Q 924 **Claustrophobia, cynophobia, and homophobia are all examples of _____.**
Q 925 **In order for a fear of common events or objects to be considered a phobia, it must be both _____ and _____.**	Q 926 **Does everybody who has a panic attack go on to develop Panic Disorder?**
Q 927 **What are some common experiences of someone experiencing a panic attack?**	Q 928 **depersonalization disorder**

A 921 Threat Hypervigilance / Uncertainty Intolerance	A 922 generalized anxiety disorder
A 923 post-traumatic stress disorder	A 924 specific phobias: specific objects or situations that provoke anxiety.
A 925 persistent irrational	A 926 No. Most people who have had a panic attack do not develop Panic Disorder. / 3-6% of people have had a panic attack.
A 927 Shortness of breath a sensation of heart beating too quickly fear of death sharp pain in chest or stomach nausea depersonalization fear of going crazy shaking sweating and dizziness.	A 928 This is a mental illness in which the patient may feel as though s/he is living outside his/her body but still retains contact with reality.

Q 929

Which psychological disorder is characterized by physical symptoms without root in actual physical causes?

Q 930

Conversion disorder and hypochondriasis both are what type of disorder?

Q 931

What is the lethality scale?

Q 932

Dissociative disorders are characterized either by a _____ of memory or a(n) _____ sense of identity.

Q 933

When someone is unable to remember things, but there is no physiological basis for the memory disruption, he is said to be afflicted with what kind of amnesia?

Q 934

In a dissociative fugue state, one first experiences a sudden and complete loss of identity which contributes to a sudden move far away from their place of origin. What happens after this loss?

Q 935

Is the validity of the diagnosis of Dissociative Identity Disorder (DID: previously known as Multiple Personality Disorder,) universally accepted?

Q 936

List some of the characteristics of attention-deficit/hyperactivity disorder (ADD/HD)

A 929 somatoform disorder	A 930 Somatoform disorder
A 931 The lethality scale is a set of criteria used to assess the likelihood of an individual committing suicide.	A 932 dysfunction altered
A 933 dissociative amnesia	A 934 the sufferer will assume a new identity because he (or she) does not remember his (or her) old identity
A 935 No. / The validity of DID is highly controversial. Some psychologists do not consider DID a true disorder but rather a culture-bound manifestation of one or more other disorders.	A 936 often diagnosed in childhood / inability to focus on demanding tasks / lack of organization / problems adhering to instructions / excessive movement / impulsivity

Q 937 Tourette's disorder is characterized by _____ and _____.	Q 938 What is the difference between retrograde and anterograde amnesia?
Q 939 What are the two main types of amnesia?	Q 940 What three ethologists shared the Nobel prize in 1973?
Q 941 Ethology is the study of _____ behaviors.	Q 942 What did Charles Darwin believe was instrumental to evolution?
Q 943 Who was the founder of ethology research?	Q 944 What subjects within ethology is Konrad Lorenz known for?

A 937 motor tics vocal tics	A 938 With retrograde amnesia one loses memories that occurred before the traumatic event with anterograde amnesia one loses memories occurring after the traumatic event.
A 939 anterograde / retrograde	A 940 Konrad Lorenz Nikolaas Tinbergen and Karl von Frisch
A 941 animal	A 942 natural selection
A 943 Konrad Lorenz	A 944 animal aggression / imprinting / releasing stimuli / fixed action patterns

Q 945

Why did Konrad Lorenz believe animal aggression was innate?

Q 946

Who do baby birds think is their mommy?

Q 947

According to Konrad Lorenz (and further supported by the research of Nikolaas Tinbergen), what triggered fixed action patterns?

Q 948

What is a fixed action pattern?

Q 949

What are the four characteristics of fixed action patterns?

Q 950

Following Konrad Lorenz's earlier research, what did Nikolaas Tinbergen's research focus on?

Q 951

What is a supernormal sign stimulus?

Q 952

Who discovered that honeybees communicate through dance?

A 945 He believed based on natural selection that aggression in animals ensured that the strongest in a species survived passing on their genes to future generations and was therefore instinctual.	A 946 Konrad Lorenz found that baby birds (and some other species) form an attachment to the first moving object they see after birth. This is called imprinting.
A 947 releasing stimuli (or sign stimuli or simply releases)	A 948 It is a chain of behaviors or events within a species brought on by releasing stimuli.
A 949 uniformity / performed by most of a species / more complex than reflexes / unstoppable once they have started	A 950 releasing stimuli / Tinbergen made models and used them in natural settings to observe the behaviors of animals.
A 951 It is an artificial releasing stimulus whose effect is greater than the naturally occurring releasing stimulus.	A 952 Karl von Frisch

Q 953 **Who coined the term "fight or flight"?**	Q 954 **After the fight or flight response, what happens to the body, according to Walter Cannon?**
Q 955 **What is the term for a molecular unit of heredity?**	Q 956 **How many chromosomes are in the nucleus of a human cell?**
Q 957 **What are gametes and how do they differ from other human cells?**	Q 958 **Are zygotes haploids or diploids? Why?**
Q 959 **What is a genotype?**	Q 960 **What is an allele?**

A 953	A 954
Walter Cannon	The body self-regulates to return to homeostasis.
A 955	**A 956**
gene / Genes are made of DNA and RNA molecules and are carried in chromosomes	23 pairs
A 957	**A 958**
In humans gametes are the sperm and ovum. / While human cells have 23 pairs of chromosomes (making them diploids) gametes only have 23 single chromosomes (making them haploids).	diploids / When the gametes from parents meet in the fertilized egg cell the 23 single chromosomes become paired making the zygote a diploid.
A 959	**A 960**
the entirety of a genetic cell's makeup / The genotype includes both dominant and recessive genes	It is any particular version of a gene including possible variations for each dominant and recessive gene (dominant-dominant dominant-recessive or recessive-recessive).

Q 961 **The sum of your physical characteristics is also known as what?**	Q 962 **What idea is central to the theory of evolution?**
Q 963 **What is natural selection?**	Q 964 **What does genetic drift refer to?**
Q 965 **What are reproduction and the furthering of genes called in terms of evolution?**	Q 966 **Organisms or animals that are concerned with furthering the entire species rather than just themselves are favoring what?**
Q 967 **The desire to protect your own genes (and thus, the genes of your family) is known as what?**	Q 968 **What are the characteristics of innate or instinctual behaviors?**

A 961	A 962
your phenotype	natural selection
A 963 It is the idea that organisms or species are more likely to survive if they adapt to fit their environment.	**A 964** It refers to the genotypic pruning or flourishing within a population through generations.
A 965 fitness	**A 966** inclusive fitness
A 967 kin selection / Inclusive fitness is born of kin selection.	**A 968** not reliant on learning or experience / relatively consistent throughout the species even initially / exist in all members of a species

Q 969 **What is the evolutionary purpose of a biological clock?**	Q 970 **What time period do circadian rhythms revolve around?**
Q 971 **What behaviors must occur to attract a member of the same species and mate?**	Q 972 **What is estrus?**
Q 973 **How has evolution discouraged inbreeding?**	Q 974 **How is mimicry evolutionarily beneficial?**
Q 975 **What is instinctive drift?**	Q 976 **What are pheromones?**

A 969	A 970
Biological clocks keep an organism in step with its environment.	one day (24 hours) cycles

A 971	A 972
courting	Estrus is the period of time when a female animal is receptive to sex for mating. This is commonly referred to as being "in heat."

A 973	A 974
Many animals from the same family have similar markings so potential suitors know to choose mates with different markings from their own.	Mimicry allows one species of animal to look/sound/smell like another species to protect themselves from harm.

A 975	A 976
When an animal forsakes conditioned responses in favor of instinctive responses.	Believed to be a form of primitive communication between animals pheromones are sensed by another's vomeronasal organ and chemically convey certain emotions like fear.

Q 977	Q 978
There are four types of reproductive isolating mechanisms, which prevent interbreeding between different (but potentially compatible) species. What are they?	**What is mechanical isolation?**

Q 979	Q 980
What type of isolation prevents one species from responding to the courting rituals of another species, preventing interbreeding?	**How does geographic isolation prevent interbreeding?**

Q 981	Q 982
Different but similar species breeding at different times in the year to prevent interbreeding is called what?	While some behaviors are innate, psychologists and ethologists agree that there is a _____ where an organism is receptive or vulnerable to learning.

Q 983	Q 984
Though related, how do the theories of natural selection and sexual selection differ?	**Choosing a stud horse to breed with a female horse to produce a strong racing horse is called what?**

A 977	A 978
mechanical isolation / behavioral isolation / geographic isolation / isolation by season	Two species have reproductively incompatible genitals.

A 979	A 980
behavioral isolation	Different species breed in different physical locations so they are unlikely to interbreed.

A 981	A 982
isolation by season	critical period (or sensitive period) / Ex: baby chicks imprinting on the first moving object they see upon birth unable to reverse it later in life.

A 983	A 984
Natural selection is concerned with the fight to live to prevent death. Sexual selection is concerned with the fight to reproduce and continue the bloodline.	selective breeding

Q 985	Q 986
How do scouting bees navigate?	How does a queen bee prevent other female bees in the hive from reproducing?

Q 987	Q 988
In beehives, who mates with the queen?	How do bees know which flowers to gather nectar from?

Q 989	Q 990
What are different "compasses" some animals (notably birds and bees) use to navigate?	How is atmospheric pressure aid to navigation?

Q 991	Q 992
Pigeons and bees are believed to sense the _____ forces of the earth, which aids navigation.	How can celestial bodies like the sun and stars aid navigation?

A 985 They use simple landmarks magnetic fields polarized light and the position of the sun to navigate.	A 986 She secretes a chemical to suppress their ovaries so only she lays eggs. / When a new queen bee emerges the old queen bee leaves the hive.
A 987 Male bees called drones to mate with the queen. Year-to-year bees mate in the same location.	A 988 Bees can see honeyguides on flowers that humans can not since they can see ultraviolet light invisible to humans.
A 989 atmospheric pressure / infrasound / magnetic sense / sun compass / star compass / polarized light / echolocation	A 990 It alerts animals (like pigeons) to changes in altitude.
A 991 magnetic	A 992 These objects serve as landmarks for some birds and bees.

Q 993

How can the sun help bees navigate on even a cloudy day?

Q 994

Do owls use echolocation?

Q 995

What was Wolfgang Kö,hler famous for?

Q 996

What are three major topics Harry Harlow used to study with rhesus monkeys?

Q 997

What did Harlow's studies on social isolation show about monkeys?

Q 998

Describe Harlow's theory of "learning to learn."

Q 999

What are the three prongs of Edward Thorndike's instrumental learning theory?

Q 1000

How do cross-fostering experiments help glean whether traits are due to nature or nurture?

A 993 Bees have the ability to see polarized light which helps detect the position of the sun and help plot a path to their destination.	A 994 no / They use regular hearing but their ears are asymmetrical which allows sound entering the ears at different times to help pinpoint the location of objects.
A 995 his studies on chimpanzees and insight learning	A 996 social isolation / contact comfort / learning to learn
A 997 Monkeys raised in isolation were never socialized so when they were around other monkeys they did not act normally particularly with sexual and maternal behaviors.	A 998 As monkeys increased their total learning experiences they were able to learn novel things more quickly.
A 999 trial error and accidental success	A 1000 Siblings are separated at birth and raised by different parents then compared to see what traits persisted suggesting heredity and which traits differed suggesting environment.

Q 1001	Q 1002
What was Eric Kandel's contribution to the concept of plasticity?	**What did Keller and Marion Breland find when they tried to teach a raccoon to deposit coins in a piggy bank?**
Q 1003 **Ethology now mainly rests within the realm of sociobiology. Who is the most recognized sociobiologist?**	Q
Q	Q
Q	Q

A 1001	A 1002
Kandel studied the sea slug Aplysia and showed that learning actually changed the synapses and neural pathways of the slug supporting the idea of neural plasticity.	They observed the raccoon treating the coins like they would crayfish trying to remove a shell. This showed an instinctual drift meaning the raccoon couldn't help behaving instinctually.
A 1003	A
E.O. Wilson / Wilson believes behavior is formed by the mingling of environment and genetics.	
A	A
A	A